Your Ultimate Legacy

Your Ultimate Legacy:

How You Can Create, Expand, Enjoy and Sell A <u>Purposeful</u> Practice.

Michael G. Stuart, JD, CPA

A **STUART LEGACY ALLIANCE** PRINTING

A **STUART LEGACY ALLIANCE** PRINTING

In affiliation with The Stuart Legacy Alliance, LLC
3701 Algonquin Road, Suite 260
Rolling Meadows, Illinois 60008

Cataloging-in-Publication Data is on file
with the Library of Congress

ISBN 978-0-692-47582-9

First **STUART LEGACY ALLIANCE** edition: July 2015

All trademarks are property of their respective companies.

Designed by Jennifer Hess

*I would like to dedicate this book to my children,
so that they can better understand the man I am
and the Legacy I leave them.*

Contents

FOREWORD
By Robert Lambert
Founding Partner, Samurai Business Group, LLC

I'm thrilled to write the introduction to this book for Michael, who I'm honored to have as a valued friend, colleague, confidant and my estate attorney. I've also had the privilege to have him as a client, who I've mentored and coached through our Samurai business development process. As a matter of fact, he's been one of our most successful clients because he's a continuous learner, implements what he's learned and is serious about being the best he can be.

I've worked for Global 50 and Fortune 500 companies and founded four successful entrepreneurial firms in my career. In my opinion, this book is spot on regarding growing and running a successful practice. Many of the principals and ideas are more universal and can be applied to help any business grow and eventually provide value for the families that assisted in that growth.

When I'm asked for advice from colleagues, friends, business associates, clients and entrepreneurs for starting and maintaining a successful firm, my usual advice is simply this: business is black and white, people are gray. So if you're going to have people in your business, you need to get the gray part right. That obviously applies to clients, prospects, partners, associates, etc. This book looks at those aspects of running a professional practice as a business which I believe are critical to its success.

Michael admitted to me that he's taken many other marketing and business development courses, however Samurai was the first one that taught him to think about why and how people buy rather than selling to them. The old adage, "People love to buy what they want and need... they hate to be sold." To my delight, Michael has incorporated many of the sales and marketing concepts that have stood the test of time in this book. The book is essentially about realizing that building a business is a creative effort that should not just die with the entrepreneur. It is a legacy that can last as long as the creator's vision does. It can be built and sustained, and their family can benefit from the hard work they have spent a lifetime building. Often a business owner has a vision for his or her company that lasts beyond them – maybe to their families, children and grandchildren, maybe to loyal employees and maybe to outside third parties.

The point is that the owner created value, which is what made them successful in the first place. That and being able to convey their passion and value to the people they serve in a meaningful way. The book was originally thought of because – and this is not limited to the legal profession – most professional schools don't teach this in their curriculum. So, the educated professional is sent out to start what they see as a noble calling, with only technical tools and none of the practical tools that can make the business a success.

Universally across the country, firms and businesses that are approaching their business this way have become the standard to strive for. This book gives practical examples of the things one should really think about before starting (or during) a practice, in order to create something that is enjoyable and gives great value and definition to that creation you spent a lifetime building.

I wish you great success and wisdom from reading this book.

Cheers,

Bob

Acknowledgements

This book has been the result of a wonderful collaboration between several people without whose advice and encouragement, this book could not have been written. I would like to thank my team — Linda Gale, whose invaluable insights were instrumental in formulating the ideas and processes outlined here; Bob Lambert, my friend and colleague, for his counsel and assistance; and finally, to my Marketing Director, Jennifer Hess, whose counsel, attention to detail and understanding of our practice was a huge contribution to this final product.

INTRODUCTION
WHY, WHO AND HOW

1. WHY THIS BOOK?

Lawyers have traditionally practiced on an hourly rate, with the profitability of the firm dependent on graduated stages of billings per level of employee. For example, associates will bill at a lower rate, but with a higher margin, while partners bill at a lot higher rate and a somewhat lower margin.

Ease of access to information is making it harder for that model to work. Hourly billing and billing for each associate – for every phone call, fax and paper clip – has never been easy for clients to accept. And the signs of revolt continue to spread. Larger firms working with this model often adjust the bills to mollify clients who've grown weary of escalating costs. Such finagling makes the traditional model (even) harder to manage inside the firm.

No surprise, then, that we see a trend towards a value-based system where the fee is dependent on the expected results and the value to the client.

What else is changing, or needs to be changing? In the U.S. and elsewhere, law schools instruct on how to be a good lawyer – Socratic method, technical aspects of the law, and perhaps how to avoid being sued yourself.

However, very few that I know of teach anything about the actual practice of law. I am referring to law as an enterprise and business, hence the title and subtitle of this book.

It's the sort of "guidebook" I could have used 15 or 20 years ago. The premise is that you, the enterprising lawyer, have a two-fold mission. First, you have to shape – or maintain, if you already have it – a resilient business that meets the test of monthly efficiency and profitability. And second, that your enterprise is open to becoming what I call a PURPOSEFUL law firm.

The Purposeful Movement started in Denver, led by a man whose ideas have made a powerful impact on me and hundreds of others. His outlook and methods appear in Chapters 13 and 14, where I tie this book's array of recommendations together in a way that will make you a Purposeful lawyer, family advisor and business-manager.

2. WHO THE AUDIENCE IS.

Another "tradition" is seldom mentioned: Lawyers traditionally are bad businesspeople and very few are aware of accounting and tax laws that impact their business. Although they can counsel clients on the client's position and risk levels in regard to those factors, they are lax in tending to such decisions for themselves.

That very well might be you! And "you" might be 32, dealing with some very tough supply-and-demand patterns (more on that below). Or you could be 52, a whiz at the consultation table and also in the courtroom, but besieged by personnel, marketing, or structural issues at the firm where you are supposed to be enjoying control and "success."

According to the American Bar Association and Forbes magazine, there are 202 law schools in the United States. Those schools turn out 43,500 graduates per year, and these grads in effect fight over 21,300 job openings – an imbalance that shows no signs of narrowing.

By 2020, if the enrollments don't decline, there will be an oversupply of lawyers. The market for attorneys is different now owing to these factors, and it will only get worse. And as people applying to law schools realize the job market at the other end may not be as promising as it is now, enrollments will almost certainly decline. In addition, large law firms are cutting back, small firms are merging, and there will be many more experienced lawyers competing for the same jobs. Not a particularly bright employment outlook!

You won't find any econometric tables or graphs in this book. For now, I can only recommend a doctrine made famous by Intel co-founder and 1990s CEO Andrew Grove. His best book carried a wise title: <u>Only the Paranoid Survive</u>.

And it wasn't a catchy saying offered to him by the publisher. Rather, it was his personal motto during three decades of competition in Silicon Valley.

The substance of this book is intended to offer more than survival – but you've got to start somewhere! If you're 30 and planning to leave the not-so-secure security of a large law firm, please – be thinking "survival." But I also hope you never, ever become "satisfied" with that.

3. HOW TO USE THIS BOOK.

For several months, this book was subtitled "the life-cycle of a law practice."

The beginning chapters make more sense for a man or woman of 30, now inside a large firm but thinking of how to "go independent." The middle chapters are aimed at the middle-aged lawyer and practice, because, speaking bluntly, if you want your enterprise to be worth XYZ millions by the time you start slowing down, certain changes have to be well along by your third decade in practice.

Those changes and reforms aren't easy to carry out. They are obviously less arduous if – during your thirties – you can make the practical and visionary design decisions while everything is new, or at least relatively flexible.

In any case, I plead guilty to writing a book that covers at least three decades of activity and challenges by any independent-minded legal professional in the U.S.A. Whether 28, 43 or 58, you are welcome to what you find here.

And, just so my meaning isn't missed, you are encouraged to pick and choose. In sum, go to the chapters that solve your immediate problems, and put off the larger and more amorphous matters until you have the time, space and seasoning to grapple with them earnestly.

I might also say – to the sibling or spouse of any lawyer who wonders what planet he or she has emigrated to – that this book as a friendly gift could constitute a safe and inexpensive trip back to "terra firma."

4. AS FOR THE AUTHOR.

There are times when this book will sound like a memoir, but my editor and I did our best to make it what I intended it to be – a mix of "how to" and coaching manual.

If you are looking for big-picture speculations on the State of the Law in the U.S.A., this won't be the book for you. I do touch on a few big themes – chiefly, what "Purposeful" has meant to me, my staff and our clients – but a work of this sort generally comes across as nuts and bolts, hammer and nails. And, to arrive at "Purposeful," you'll also have to function as an architect – or perhaps if you are near 50, as a radical remodeller.

Finally, unlike most every other book that attempts to convey the real world of Law as a Business, this one takes the story, and your own likely trail, right to the end of the line: Selling what will have become a great practice.

I am very appreciative of your time as a reader and especially your interest in what this book tries to do. After I "ease out" of my own practice, I might be a good candidate to speak to, and take a few hard-hitting questions from, your professional society or organization (you'll find contact info on the back page of this book).

Whatever you do and don't do with the principles, methods and behaviors that follow, I feel sure you will end up with a healthy sense of innovation and ownership – not to mention happier clients and higher profit margins.

Michael G. Stuart
Rolling Meadows, Illinois
March 28, 2015

CHAPTER 1
LOCATION AS A BIG PART OF VOCATION

When I got the offer to work at Coopers & Lybrand in Portland, Oregon, I was struck to find myself in one of the most beautiful places in the world. If you like being outdoors, Portland is great. (So is Seattle, for that matter, with the added benefit of no state income tax!) I could make a great living at the firm, learn a great deal, and still be near enough to the activities that make life enjoyable.

But how much "enjoy" time would be on hand with a billable-time obligation stretching to 2,000 hours per year? Rude awakening: To bill 2,000 hours, a lawyer at that point had to work 2,500 to 3,000 hours because some of the time had to be written off and a certain amount of non-billable time (for administration and the like) further skewed the mix.

In any case, Coopers & Lybrand in Portland was a superb training ground. I was blessed to learn from top people in the field about estate planning, business planning and exit planning. And it gave me the opportunity to earn my CPA – invaluable for a tax lawyer. All these things gave me a strong background in the technical aspects of my chosen career.

The location decision had been "solved" – pretty much in passing – by the job I had taken, which lasted three years. Then it came time to really think about location in its own right, using a decades-long perspective.

I never really thought about what it would be like practicing on my own and having to do all the things to run a successful practice. That early deficit really explains the entire first half of this book. But my editor said to keep the chapters short and make them sequential – in terms of how your life as a man or woman of the law is likely to develop – and this first one will make the most sense to someone between the ages of 25 and 35.

In an established firm, your clients in effect are your bosses and colleagues. When you own your own firm, you get to recruit – recruit the clients, that is. Staying in Portland – but becoming independent and leaving Coopers & Lybrand – entailed making the location decision all over again. How many people did I know in Portland who would help grow a practice?

Staying in New York, I would have had a built-in network of contacts. My father had practiced law in lower Manhattan for several years, and even though his practice died with him in 1962, I could have reconnected with his friends and clients and gotten a leg up on the networking.

But New York was very competitive and it would be difficult to start and keep a practice, so Portland would be a good alternative – that's what I thought.

The metropolitan area of Portland has about one million residents – versus many times that in NYC. But it's easy to confuse oneself with statistics, assuming they are big enough. What I didn't realize is that there were something like 60,000 lawyers practicing in the state, mostly in Northern Oregon and the Portland area, so the available pool of prospective clients was more limited.

It won't hurt to dwell on that phrase – "the available pool of prospective clients." You'll never get the statistic down cold, but any diligent estimate is better than intuition and wishful thinking. When you are looking for a place to set up shop, you should think about that "pool" – who you know that you can begin networking with versus the number of tangible rivals.

This decision also involves the physical location of the practice. Locating your shop on Oregon's Pacific Coast – which requires a 60-mile drive due west from any of the cities on Interstate 5, including

Portland, Salem and Corvallis – would make your off-hours rejuvenating and at times magical.

But to make that drive more than once or twice per week – on two-lane highways favored by logging trucks, and with walls of thick evergreens shutting out the sun – will get old fast. And you will be doing much driving because a law practice on the coast of Oregon will severely limit your pool of clients.

Think about the type of "life/work balance" you want to maintain. Do you want to work 40 hours a week and possibly limit your income in order to spend more time with your family and the things you enjoy? Or are you willing to put in more time at work to increase your income? Working in a large firm is financially rewarding, but the demands on your time will be heavy, leaving less time to do the things you enjoy outside of work.

I spent about 10 years in Portland practicing law and then moved to Chicago, rather than New York City, in the late 1980s.

Since this book is beginning with the early days of an independent law practice, the next realm to explore is networking. For anyone who is self-employed, networking is a lifetime obligation. But the time when it's most needed – when you move from being an employee to an autonomous actor –

is also the time when it's most difficult to do that networking effectively.

CHAPTER 2
NETWORKING (DURING THE EARLY YEARS)

Anyone who has gotten through law school without having their extroversion beaten out of them must be quite a "social animal." But simply meeting new people will not have clients beating a path to your door. Nor do friendly encounters with wealth advisors guarantee they will open up their book and share two or three good prospects you can pay a respectful visit to next week.

When I first started getting out and about in the Portland area, I would meet as many potential referral sources as I could. Our conversations centered on the outlook that they should be referring me to their clients because I had a different way, a better way, to help those clients. This may have been true – in other words, my "way" might really have been a leap they'd need to make – but it is ludicrous to think that you would meet someone today and they would start referring you business next week.

I heard my father say it, and probably his father before him as well, but it still applies: "People won't care how much you know until they know how much you care." They need to get to know, like and trust you before they refer you. And that referral might not happen even after "like" and "trust" have become facts; it could take another year, or three, beyond that. And so you have to be lodged in their minds when the situation arises that causes them to need your particular expertise. This is often called Top of Mind Awareness, or "TOMA."

So how does one achieve that? The best attitude and policy is: Give before you get. If you show someone that you truly are trying to help advance their career, it will come back many times over in business to the firm. So you need to find people you know, like and trust – people you would feel comfortable referring clients to – and offer to help them wholeheartedly and sincerely in any way you can.

Maybe you can't refer them a prospect right away, but maybe you can connect them to others who can help. As I developed my network, people looked to me as a "connector" – that's one of three business "types" in Malcolm Gladwell's famous book The Tipping Point – who has contacts that might offer an advisor the opportunity to win more clients.

Not every person you meet will fall into the "know, like, trust" category. Initially, you might not even have many referral sources or advisors with whom to start the process. In that case, I would make a list of everyone I knew, family and friends, and make time to go talk with them. Have a well-structured outline of what you want to convey – I call it "the story," covering why you started the practice and what types of cases you'd be thrilled to work on.

Then ask how you could help them. Simple question, and it often leads to profound answers (and you'll never get in trouble for having asked). You'd be amazed at how many people fail to offer help in whatever form is appropriate; and, precisely because those individuals miss the chance to follow through in that manner, your doing so will be very refreshing and keep you Top of Mind.

Even if you can't help them with anything that week or that month, your contacts will very much appreciate your asking the question. Something could occur to them later on which they need help, and you would keep that door open by telling them "do not hesitate to contact me" – even if it looks to be outside your current area of expertise.

When I decided to make network-style marketing the center of my marketing efforts, I made a list of all the people who had referred me business in the past two years and made it a point to set up meetings with them again to ask their advice. These are people I respected for their business acumen and counsel over the years. My exact inquiries:

a) What was it about me or our firm that made you refer us in the first place?

b) What was the client's reaction to engaging our firm?

c) What was the advisor's reaction to our process?

d) What worked and what didn't?

e) What could we do better and how?

f) What was the biggest problem the advisor had with attorneys generally?

g) What was the biggest problem the advisor had with our firm?

Then – this is the clincher – the request was made for five people they thought might be interested in having a similar chat. I was more than likely to trust anyone they recommended spending time with. After all, since these were people I trusted, it was a good bet that they surrounded themselves with others who operated pretty much the way they did.

Obtaining such insights will help make your practice the best it can be, wouldn't you say?

It was slow at first, but I met some excellent

connectors that referred me people who were willing to help. Usually I didn't start out the conversation inquiring as to how they could help. As a matter of fact, I rarely mentioned it at any point during our talk. Rather, I asked how I could help them. I knew I could refer them a client and they would be very happy to have me do so, but was there any additional way I could help them? Was there anyone in my network who could advance their career, client list or pet project? Who were the people who referred them the most clients?

I knew that I would meet some pretty interesting individuals who would know the kind of people I wanted as clients. This led to having me be TOMA with them, so when a client came before them who might need my services, it was more likely that they would think of me when making that referral.

Professional and other networking groups are a good way to get known in the community and with your peers. Choose wisely, because it can get out of hand very quickly.

At first I took a "shotgun" approach: Join every organization in which I had a contact, or that someone had touted to me, and meet as many people as possible. What I found is that many of the organizations were nothing more than people getting together to hand out as many business cards as possible. You will run yourself ragged going to such meetings. Choose groups that will leverage your time and that you enjoy being a part of.

I chose settings where I sincerely enjoyed most of the people involved in the group – individuals with a similar mindset in terms of "give before you get" and whom I truly liked as people and would consider working with.

I joined the local estate-planning councils, which are comprised of attorneys, accountants and financial professionals, and found the educational dimension of their programs very informative. Such councils generally meet once a month as opposed to weekly. Remember that any organization that requires a weekly meeting tends to be a serious time and energy obligation; and, if you can't make every meeting, that's a disservice to you and those in the group.

Also, get involved in groups whose mission or philosophy is one with which you agree. Don't just go to join. Get involved if you can or want to, serve on committees or – yes, I am serious – run for office. Initially in your career, you will have the time to do this and it will get you known. As the practice grows, your time will be more limited, but you will be seen as a leader and someone to be sought out.

I have had several colleagues who decided to run for office and, even though they didn't win, they thought the experience very beneficial. It can be a noble calling. It also takes a great deal of work, requires a great deal of face time with the public, opens your private life to scrutiny, and can take a toll on your personal relationships.

A wise course is to set aside becoming Governor or Senator, even in your thirties. But the city council, the board of education and the board of elections tend to be part-time roles with decent levels of responsibility and visibility.

Serving on your church or synagogue board, or with groups like the Jaycees and Lions Club – also worth considering. There are many civic groups out there. Find one that appeals to you and your involvement with the community and lend a hand.

CHAPTER 3
SELF-KNOWLEDGE: HOW ARE YOU?

It's Week One, and for a time you will be doing everything in the firm, starting with making sure the new (and especially the used) furniture is placed right. The firm is you, and you are the firm. If there were an organization chart – one with pictures – your face would be there next to every job title.

We'll get to hiring staff in a moment, but first: You'll need to become clear on what is effective for you – your work style, your tolerance for getting the work done, the type of people you like to be around, and perhaps the type you might need to have around, whether you "like" them or not.

If you have just left a more traditional firm, you are well aware of what you didn't like about that particular enterprise. You opted to leave that enterprise and now, suddenly, you are 100% of a brand new enterprise. Not in terms of equity, but definitely in terms of situational control, you'll soon have to "give away" (or loan) parts of your daily operation to others. And those people deserve to know, in their own "first week," how you will be operating.

Is your style to get things done last minute, or do you like to get things done more calmly and make sure you have plenty of time to review? Can staff look to you as a "coach" and master problem-solver? Or, at the opposite extreme, do you like to do your own work while "expecting" everyone else to handle their tasks and zones intuitively?

To find out your skill set, which of course influences hiring, turn to assessment tools such as the "DiSC" analysis or the Kolbe tests. These are not IQ tests; rather, they assess how you work and how you will be able to work with others.

The Kolbe test pegged me as a Quick Start. That means that I am very entrepreneurial, have many things playing out at once, have a lot of new ideas, and like to meet with people to make things happen.

Over the years, I also learned to follow through with those ideas and acquired the discipline to get things done. And yet – I recognize that "follow-through" is not my true skill. My executive assistant on the other hand is a great Follow-Through person who completes tasks in an orderly and efficient manner without too much direction from me.

I opted to hire an executive assistant rather than a receptionist. The need was for someone who could do more than be pleasant and handle phone calls. Since this would be the first "face" of the firm when dealing with clients, I had to find someone who was outstanding on the phone, could establish rapport right away, and put clients or prospective clients at ease the moment they walked into the office.

At first, she was a little unsure of what I wanted, and quite frankly, I was more stern with her than I needed to be. That is a mistake common to Quick-Starts and other self-directed individuals who need trial and error to appreciate the value of trust and communication. In a phrase: Explain, Don't Exclaim.

In learning to work with this new E.A., I was being a boss – and only a boss – rather than a team member. When you stop and think of it, your immediate assistant doesn't just support your work, you also need to support theirs. You might be the rainmaker bringing in new clients, but your second in command is the one who coordinates schedules and sets up the meeting.

When she first came on board, I still wanted to control everything – from calendaring appointments to meeting with clients to doing the work. In order to get past that M.O., I needed some kind of operational demand where my interventionist tendency would cause grief if not chaos.

Soon after the E.A. joined the firm, our lease was up. The decision had already been made to take a slightly larger space in the same building. And I was on the phone – not working with clients, but trying to coordinate the transfer of our phone and computer systems. The E.A. saw me struggling with that and knew that client work was being neglected. So she said: "Stop doing that and go work on the client files. Phones, computers, and moving the office are my job."

A great eye-opener, don't you think? Have you ever had an associate make a similar point to you? I hope you did not get defensive; more likely, you should have given him or her a bonus – not on the spot, but later that week.

She demonstrated the willingness to step up to the plate and relieve me of busy work that wasn't advancing the cash flow of the firm. I reluctantly gave in. When moving day arrived, we were in the new office and operating by 10 a.m. – and I had not lifted a box. The team pulled together, hired movers for the furniture and got the systems all in place without me lifting a finger!

That taught me a great lesson about delegation:

FIND THE RIGHT PERSON and DELEGATE
ALL EXCEPT YOUR UNIQUE TALENTS AND
ABILITY.

Entrepreneurs are rugged individualists who can
do anything that needs to be done. But unless the
mailing has to go out by 3 p.m. and you feel like
using the "stuffing party" to swap stories with your
staff, do we really need to fold the letters and apply
the stamps? Or deal with the phone company or IT
operatives in order to get systems running?

Again, the point is: Find out what you do best
and delegate almost everything else.

As you mature in the practice, you will find there
are things you are more skilled at – which are also
more profitable and beneficial to the firm – than
worrying about the more mundane tasks. Furthermore, you will likely find that those mundane tasks
you were "merely competent at" can probably be
completed by someone else more effectively and
profitably for the firm.

The more cases you work on, the more difficult
it will be for you to do everything, and the more
stress and pressure you will be under. Learn how to

delegate those things you don't do well, and have a procedure that allows you to easily review and assign projects to trusted colleagues, ensuring the work gets done efficiently, correctly and on a timely basis.

The next chapter says more about hiring and looks at creating a desirable office culture – two more challenges that require self-knowledge.

CHAPTER 4
OFFICE: CULTURE AND ASSOCIATES

For most of the time since 2008, the job market has been tight and many lawyers are looking for jobs. One would think this favors you as their potential employer. On the other hand, many have been downsized from larger firms; and, a result, they carry some expectations about workload and salary that exceed your ability to pay, at least during these early years.

In my experience, younger lawyers have great expectations that may not be borne out in their levels of experience and education. Lawyers who graduated from prestigious schools or were top in their class are probably going to get hired by the big firms or will have higher expectations.

Simply put, going out and searching for lawyers is very hard. And Chapter 10 will have much more to say about this tough but necessary part of growing your enterprise. For now, let's look at hiring everyone else.

You want to choose people who can blend into your corporate culture and can form a team that moves in the same direction as you. That means you first have to determine what your firm's culture and goals will be.

For example, if you value integrity and want the team to function accordingly – owning up to mistakes, finding ways to solve them without blame, and creating the best experience for the client – that differs from a team culture that strives chiefly to bring in money. (Money is important, indeed essential, but it is not the only value that is important.)

Ask applicants questions that are in line with your goals and office culture. In fact, that set of questions ought to be put to each applicant – no matter what the job – because everyone will be contributing to the culture and the firm's goals. You could go through several interviews before you meet the right person, and certainly personal chemistry has a great deal to do with it.

Also, consider the position for which you are interviewing. A receptionist has to have a pleasant speaking voice and like to talk to people on the phone. You would be surprised how many people apply for a specific job, and the interview process reveals that they are either overqualified or simply lack the skills required to perform that job.

And that's another word – "job" – that is less

than encouraging. I prefer to think that people are entering a career when they come into our firm. And since we are a small office, everyone's contribution to the progress of the firm is key. In the end, the "buck stops on my desk" because ultimately the team will defer to me. Even so, when they become involved in the process, not just as implementers but also as advisors, the end result is far better and everyone is usually on board with the decision or method of moving forward.

From the receptionist to the managing partner in the firm, everyone can be a marketer for your services. Encourage them to bring in business and reward them financially for doing so. Get them all business cards and reward them for taking initiatives to bring in business. One thing I have learned is that the reach of a firm's marketing expands exponentially when there is more than one person going out and preaching the virtues of that enterprise.

Remember, Chapter 10 will cover the hiring and managing of lawyers. For now, let's survey the rest of the team and the office culture...

PARALEGALS.

What skills will a person need for the position you are trying to fill? Try to outline the duties that the ideal new person should have and build the ideal job description. Are the skills more technical than administrative? Is the person going to have client contact? Are you looking for someone to be in the back office grinding out work, or are they expected to have some rainmaking duties? Do they need to have a number of years of technical experience? If so, in what areas, and how do you verify that?

When I first got to the point that I knew I needed help, I really didn't understand the hiring process and tried to train a secretary who had little law firm experience. I wound up spending a lot of time training her, and in the end, I realized the personality differences made a long-term relationship impossible.

After that, I hired a paralegal with whom I had worked in a previous firm. Initially, she was effective, but ended up making the process more difficult than it had to be. I found out after we started working together that her personality was such that collaborating as a true team was difficult. When she came in and said she was leaving for another firm, that news was no surprise, and I knew that as a firm we would be okay. But I also realized that I needed to decide if the time was right to hire a lawyer.

Still, I continued with the paralegal search. I hired a recruiter that a colleague had recommended to me, and they interviewed my E.A. and myself as to what type of person we were looking for. They were very thorough, prepared the job description, and screened the applicants. I highly recommend this as a procedure because you will probably get a lot of resumes for the advertised position, and you won't have the time or the inclination to go through them all. And, although you are the HR department, you were not trained as an HR person. Delegate to those who can do those functions better than you.

That being said, we narrowed the field to three candidates and selected one who had a few years of experience. And he was great! A wonderful draftsman, knowledgeable, intuitive, and technically very savvy. He could multi-task with the best of them and, in a small office that really counts.

What he lacked was the drive to market and be out in the rainmaker's role. He was great at the back office tasks and kept things running, but we needed more than that. I had many discussions with him about his role in the firm, and we mutually decided that he was not the asset that the firm needed.

Then I tried hiring a lawyer, and found that lawyers – even the relative newbies – felt that they had more to offer than they in fact did.

Finally, I decided to hire a good paralegal to

round out the technical things that needed to be done in the office. As I mentioned before, the first time I hired a paralegal, I went to someone with whom I had worked before and knew she was looking for a different position. We really didn't have a process to hire someone, or integrate them into the firm culture, but I needed someone to help me with the workload, and I figured she was a known quantity.

I kept her on longer than I should have because she got the work done efficiently, but she caused tension with others in the firm, and that drew away from the team concept and the firm culture. In truth, there was hardly a "team" at that point, merely people who worked in the same office. And I realized that for the firm to thrive, there had to be a commitment from all of us to build the firm.

Ultimately, after some bad luck in hiring lawyers, I returned to the paralegal search. My thought was that a paralegal would better fit the needs of our firm – we needed someone to handle the back-office work, and the right paralegal could probably do that more efficiently than a lawyer. Additionally, there would be very little risk of the paralegal taking clients if they sought greener pastures.

I put an ad in the various papers and law schools

searching for the right candidate. We received nine responses, and I decided to do the first round of interviews as a group. We got the nine people into a conference room, and I had my list of questions.

The interesting thing was the variety of people that emerged. Several were fresh out of paralegal school with their newly minted paralegal certificates in hand looking for an opportunity – any opportunity – to work in a law firm. For this part of the group, then, experience was lacking.

Most of the applicants did not have any estate-planning experience, which I felt was critical for the type of work they would be required to do and the maturity of the firm. Three were lawyers and a little older in age, but they had either left firms for one reason or another or were looking to supplement their income in retirement. They did not seem to have a fire in their belly to help me and the firm grow.

One candidate was fresh out of law school, had no experience at all (I learned that later), but he hadn't been admitted to the bar yet. The thing that intrigued me about him was his desire and drive. He was committed to making the firm better and said he would do anything it took to do so. He was willing to start at the ground floor and learn.

I took a chance, and although he was young and inexperienced, I felt I could teach him the ropes. Even though it would take six months or a year, I would have someone in the firm who both understood my strategies and could think like a lawyer. Maybe he could be a partner some day! I still think it was a good choice. Though he has much to learn, he is an active member of the team and strives every day to live within the firm culture and advance our progress. Truly, he is a team player.

I guess the moral of the story is that you need to identify what skills are required for the position, and recognize the degree of oversight you'll need to demonstrate once you hire this person. If they are younger or inexperienced, they may be more eager, but you will have to spend more time training them. In the end, you could have a great team player and colleague by going this route. On the other hand, if you hire an experienced paralegal, they can be worth their weight in gold if they fit into the culture you've developed within your firm.

And hiring a lawyer requires that you are aware that you could be training your competition, or you need to figure out a way to overcome that possibility. Another lawyer also adds to the continuing education and malpractice premiums along with other payroll costs that will increase.

Just remember to choose wisely and remind yourself that sometimes what is on paper isn't enough. Get to know the person behind the resume.

MEETINGS AND PARTIES.

For several reasons, I recommend weekly team meetings. As you get busier, you will not be able to handle every little detail in the office or manage the "business" of practicing. You will have to delegate projects to others while maintaining the responsibility of ensuring everything is on track.

I suggest you implement a process that allows you to oversee everything you work on. We use a process which lists every pending project plus the estimated fees to be received and when. That way, I can project the cash flows for the business and nothing will get lost on someone's desk. All the work will get done and you will be better able to keep in touch with your clients. In a small office it also serves as a way to get closer to your team and help you develop a strong team culture.

Other events are worth your consideration. One is holiday parties for the team and their spouses or current significant others We have had some wonderful Christmas parties that promote goodwill, camaraderie, and help foster that team attitude and culture. Your team works hard, and you should recognize that and reward them occasionally with a significant event that honors them in some way. Some firms depending on the size, also have "employee of the month" contests honoring those employees who demonstrate the firm culture, enhance the client experience, or develop a new process that saves time or money. Get creative – remember this is your practice! Make it fun.

EVENTS FOR CLIENTS.

As the firm starts becoming more efficient and profitable, I would also consider having an event for clients. As you are taking client information, you can ask what things they like to do. For example, as part of our regular client intake we started asking clients about the hobbies they enjoy when they are not working. Is it golf, travel, wine-tasting or skiing? Whatever gets enough votes, engineer an event around that – a golf outing with two to seven people, a wine-tasting for a small group – and just enjoy their company and get to know them. Have no agenda beyond friendly socializing and I guarantee that all of you will be talking about it for months.

We have an event every year to honor our clients

featuring a nice dinner at a local upscale restaurant. It started as a lark, but now usually over 100 clients attend, and we learn some of the most wonderful stories about the clients' families. Through this annual event, we wind up bonding closer to the clients and handful of advisors we invite. It is a wonderful way to keep in touch, and we try to keep it low-key without too much technical information so clients don't get bored.

When I first started having the event, I used to give a year-end tax update, and when the law was changing, I felt the clients wanted to hear that. Then we learned that our clients came to see the team and weren't so interested in the technical aspects of the law. So, instead of having a 30-minute presentation that could be perceived as a sales pitch, we now instead thank everyone for coming, honor the staff for their help during the year, and limit it to about a 15-minute presentation of thanksgiving.

CHAPTER 5
OFFICE: PROPS, FEATURES AND SPACE

The great thing about leaving the "big" law firm is that you get to reinvent everything – everything except your core values, that is – from the ground up. The not-so-great thing is that reinvention can be hard.

But this next set of decisions are unique in that they require an initial intense focus, after which you can forget about them for a good long while, taking into account creativity and functionality, and get back to the more exciting details of running your practice.

DESK.

At first, you will have a low budget and there is plenty of high quality used office furniture that will serve your needs. Even after three years, Jeff Bezos and his Amazon colleagues had "desks" made up of old doors laid sideways on various props. That's well and good, but their customers were coming to them via the still new Internet, not walking in for a chat about the deepest of personal matters. How will your own visitors feel? What sensations will they tend to have coming through your door? And how will you feel, spending the day at work, even when you have no visitors?

Early on, I decided to buy a "new" desk, and apply a few parameters. Because I am a very visual person, my desk had to be large enough to lay things out so I could see them. The original desk I bought was beautiful – a discontinued radial-arm model with a 3' x 6' desktop. Unfortunately, it didn't come apart and it was solid oak about two inches thick. The first time I moved to a new office, it was a pain. Later, I went for a new desk "modular" system that could be rearranged based on the configuration of the office.

Because you will eventually switch offices, flexibility in your working environment is important. One thing to think about is the comfort level for you and your clients. Some of the older desks have overhangs in the front, so if a client is in your office and you need to sign documents, they will have space to do that. This provides the versatility of doing more business in your office rather than requiring a conference room or separate area.

Also, you want to make sure you have the space to work when your desk is loaded with papers that you don't want to move. Some of the older desks have sideboards that slide into the desk when not being used, and can be pulled out in an emergency to quickly sign a document.

Also consider the alignment of your other equipment that you like to have on-hand. For example, if you like to have your phone, computer monitor, printer, adding machine or calculator (and whatever else) near at hand, will all of those tools really fit on your desk and still give you space to work?

CHAIR.

No point in skimping here. Buy the most ergonomically comfortable chair that you can. I first got a Judge's chair with a high back, and it was very comfortable, but it lacked durability, armrest adjustments and lumbar support. You will spend much of your working life in the office sitting in that chair and you don't want to go home at night with pains in your back or arms from an improperly positioned chair – or I should say a chair that improperly positions your neck, shoulders and arms.

COMPUTER.

Whether you choose a single standalone

computer or a system that your whole office staff can access, make sure you have your desk "fitted" to sit properly at the computer. This will avoid a lot of neck and back pain when you are working late into the night. (Details about how the computer, especially the software, actually functions are covered in the next chapter.)

CONFIGURATION.

Do you need an office primarily to meet people? Sometimes you can work out deals with firms that have excess space to set up a basic office, share copiers, phone systems and fax machine. I did that for awhile and it has its advantages. We had a deal with an office-sharing group where we rented our office, but could use satellite offices when needed to meet a client who was outside that area. This worked for a time, but eventually we wanted to have our own branding and presence. Not only that, but it can get quite expensive in an office-sharing arrangement where you are paying for everything a la carte.

The satellite offices are important if your clientele is dispersed over a wide area. Remember that if you make it difficult for clients to see you, they could find someone else. One of the nice aspects about having your own office, besides the branding, is that you can decorate it. Of course, that means paying for additional furniture, couches, tables, plants and wall coverings. Because we have a Legacy practice, we decided to have wall coverings that spotlight our families. Clients have told us that the office has a warm and inviting atmosphere.

Do you need a conference room to meet with clients, will you meet them in your office or go to their homes or businesses? Remember, if you see clients in your office, that means you will need to maintain a clean and tidy work space for at least two reasons. One, the client wants to know you are a professional, and two, you need to keep other clients' work confidential. A messy office signals neither.

If you do need a conference room, again you need to consider table and chairs for that room, how many will need to be accommodated, whether you need to have speaker phone or internet access, white board, panaboard or – if you are really high tech – a TV that connects to your server, along with how the overall room will look and feel. Your budget will be a prime consideration here.

If you decide to rent space, I would suggest you hire a "tenant advocate." Again, time misspent is your enemy and anything you can do to cut down the time it takes to look at office space the better. We hired an excellent advocate, told him our wants and needs, and he negotiated on our behalf. (Because he was paid by the landlord, the result was in our price range.)

In our most recent move, the building management decided to lease space to an oncology division for an MRI unit – right next to our office – without conferring with us. In case you haven't been through an MRI, they can be very noisy and disruptive. The tenant advocate was able to negotiate a great deal with the building-owners, delivering larger space at a lower rate, plus parking and a better view as bonuses.

Best of all, we only looked at the few places that he had vetted, saving us much time in the process of getting a better rate and features.

Your office will probably need storage for files, paper and other office supplies, in addition to a copier, computer room or area, fax machine and shredder. Copiers nowadays are multi-function combination units that do copying, faxing, and connect to computers wirelessly among other things.

You should develop a system to organize your files and make your office as paperless as possible. (More on this in the next chapter.) Otherwise you will find, as we did, that paper files take up a lot of room, and it is much easier to search a computer file rather than navigate the depths of a file cabinet.

Additionally, when it comes to file-management, make sure that someone is responsible for putting the file in order after you deal with it – that means not only returning it to where it belongs, but also ensuring that the contents of the file are organized based on your standards and file naming conventions. This applies to all files in your office space, both digital and paper. By establishing a certain way the files are organized, every file you pick up will have the same things in the same place. It will drive you crazy (at least it does me) to have 10 minutes to act on something and spend an hour looking for that one document you know you created and was in the file, but – what happened to it? Set up the system and give someone else the responsibility to keep the vital reports and documents accessible.

Should your office have a galley or kitchen or someplace where associates can just take a break? This is a cost consideration along with whether there are physical offices for the attorneys, partitions, etc.

When I first took an office, I rented more space than I needed, but it had everything and I felt I would grow into it. It had a break room with refrigerator and sink for coffee and lunches, a large file room, five outside windowed offices, a large conference room – along with a classroom that seated about 25, which let us put on seminars without the expense of renting a hall or restaurant facility. As we were putting on a lot of seminars at that time, that classroom felt like an unexpected windfall.

All the same, paying for space you are not using – and in fact might never use – is a drain on cash flow. If you wind up with surplus space, look for someone to rent what you won't soon need as a way to mitigate the cost. Also, if you have more offices than you want, you may rent them out to other lawyers whose expertise may be synergistic with yours. If you want to cut costs, you may seek out collaborative practices in other areas of the law which can get you new business, and they may have extra space to rent at lower cost. Then you can negotiate for use of common services such as reception and file room space.

CHAPTER 6
INFORMATION WITHOUT INFLAMMATION

Both this and the next chapter come at "information" and "systems" in somewhat different ways. Unless you are truly the nuts-and-bolts type, my guess is you will like this approach more than the one taken in Chapter 7.

But all of it matters, and covering all the bases in both chapters will save you, your staff and best clients hundreds of hours of grief. Here goes...

FILE STRUCTURE.

Even before you open your doors, seriously consider whether you need or want paper files. Some paper-collection is unavoidable during the first few years, and of course documents pile up during and near critical meetings and judicial events. For later storage and occasional retrieval, though, you'll want to have your files scanned in an organized manner logically on the computer.

And "on the computer" these days also means backed-up somewhere. If you don't trust the so-called "cloud" services – and I still wonder how they can call it a "cloud" when in fact all the storage and servers remain on the ground! – consider investing $1,000 or so in a Drobo, and keep everything securely in-house with fail-safe protections. www.drobo.com

SECURITY IS SACROSANCT.

We are living in a time when hackers can magically – and tragically – "lock" all your firm's files and demand a ransom. Here's how a news analysis on University-based WAMU-FM described it in December 2014:

> Somebody in the office opened an email that looked legit. "It has the exact background of like PayPal," [company computer-manager Eric] Young recalls, "and it says, somebody paid you money." The employee clicked the link and out popped a red alert that took up most of the screen. It was a threat: Pay ransom to an anonymous hacker, or all the files in the company network will be encrypted – locked up with a digital key that's so strong, no one can open them ever again. The threat came with a countdown clock. Young had 72 hours and, as he tried to find solutions, the cyber-thieves were slipping into every company computer – starting with Victim No. 1 and ending in the company's servers. "Our database was encrypted and ... we lost everything we had built for 14 years."

Writer Atari Shamanic concluded his story this way, referring to Chris Morales at NSS Labs: "Ransom ware has gotten so powerful, Morales says, the hackers really do lock down victims' data... The very best defense, he says, is having a backup that's not connected to your machine in any way. Storing things on the cloud or on a USB drive that's plugged into your computer won't cut it."

AUTOMATE.

Every lawyer uses forms to help prepare for a new case. Automating the forms is key to developing a process to get things done quickly and efficiently.

Review every document carefully and don't rely on the form alone. If possible – and "if possible" doesn't mean "if convenient" – have a second lawyer or eagle-eyed friend review the document for accuracy, typos and stylistic glitches such as conflicting methods of punctuation.

There are substitutes for technical expertise, but they tend to start off cheap and wind up costing you a great deal.

CATEGORIZE.

When you are organizing the files, figure out basic categories of information that you want to keep track of on the computer. Rather than having several file folders to look through for information, create a legend of common types of files and make sure everyone knows the filing system. Before I realized this, my former assistant was keeping files on her computer, and on the server, without a naming standard.

For example: You can file something as "Jones Memo_06-06-2013" but that will organize the file differently because of the date. If someone else uses a different date format, you might be unable to easily find what you need, or it may not be in chronological order. Keeping things chronologically might not make the most sense, but you just don't want to spend your time fishing through computer or paper files to find the document you need right now for court purposes or to accommodate the IRS.

TRACK CHANGES.

Consider investing in and learning a program that can automatically update fields without having to "search and replace." This will be a great time-saver and if the original document is reviewed for technical competence, it will be easier to create new documents as they are needed, using the original as a trustworthy template. You can research software such as Hotdocs or Formtool and see if they work for you.

Keep a record for each file that identifies the changes or additions made to the document, so if it needs to be updated later, you know what special provisions were added and how they might affect any future edits.

DIGITIZE.

Some of the office-supply companies offer filing services. Among other benefits, these services allow you to automatically categorize documents as they're being scanned into the computer so everything is filed in the same way. Having some standard to lock-in consistency is important, so spend the time beforehand when you're ready to set this up.

The rest of this chapter focuses on CRM – Customer Relations Management – software. It has become the method of choice for all kinds of enterprises keep track of clients. This is one of the most crucial pieces of software you will purchase, as it will cover your prospects, advisors and clients, and most of all, your schedule!

a) What information do you want to keep track of and how will it be secure? If you keep Social Security numbers in your file (which you might need for income or estate tax returns, for example), how will you secure that information?

b) To keep in touch with clients, you will certainly need contact information, but what about the name of the individual who referred the client to you, which will be important in your networking efforts. Plus the inclusion of details such as children's names and secondary contacts – their financial advisors, CPA, insurance agent, etc. – can help you provide your clients with even better service.

c) Keeping track of special information that's unique to your clients or their situation, including document custom-ization details, EINs for entities you create and their names or related entities. For example, most attorneys use software to create documents, but the software will not typically cover all contingencies. When you modify a document to cover a particular situation, you want to be able to document that fact for at least two reasons.

First, if you need to amend or update the document later, you want to be able to be consistent and carry forward the parts you customized so that they are included in the updated document. This could be especially important in estate plans where the Trust-Creator's intent is not carried forward from document to document. If the document is ever called into question, you have the consistency of the prior documents to support the Trust-Creator's position.

Second, when you have a similar situation in the future, you will want to be able to retrieve your hard work so you don't have to reinvent the wheel. Remember, it is easier to edit than create, so keeping track of your prior genius is critical.

d) The CRM system should be robust enough to grow with you and provide the information you need over time. It should also be expandable to accommodate your needs as the practice changes. Keep track of not only the details about the client (name, address, phones, birthdays, emails, etc.) but also details like children's names, personal hobbies, and favorite vacation destinations.

Suffice it to say that gathering the knowledge when the client is in a sharing mood allows you to properly service that client. You'll be able to give advice not in a vacuum, but with a background in what the client is trying to accomplish. For example, in our practice, we keep track of typical client data like name, address, phone and email. But through the use of our CRM, we are also able to include hobbies, which attorney brought in the case, file number, client number, marital status, estate size, name of revocable trusts, advanced planning completed, physical location of the file, secondary contacts, referral sources, follow-up calls and meetings… the possibilities are endless. It's all about what has value for you and your firm.

And now for Chapter 7 – the one that became so comprehensive it had to be divided into a Preview and an Appendix. (And of course you can't find an Appendix inside a chapter...)

CHAPTER 7
SYSTEMS, RULES AND HABITS

This chapter gets at some of the same needs as the prior one did, but our original version contained some of the densest detail you're ever likely to see. Dozens upon dozens of points were being covered, mostly with one-line statements and phrases. Why? Because the whole mission of this book is to offer you an awareness of everything – everything likely to be pertinent to your firm's design, growth, management and operating principles.

At the same time, the book has to maintain its conversational feel – as opposed to sounding like a checklist for a space-shuttle launch!

And that's why we moved to Plan B. "Chapter 7" is now an outline of important topic areas, while most of the details have been moved to an Appendix (Page 123). This is my lawyer training kicking in – trying to be detailed and at the same time remain readable. Here goes. The theme is SETTING UP SYSTEMS.

- In our practice, having systems for just about everything became the most effective way to make governance and management easier.

- Not every practice can systematize processes, but the Appendix shows a few of the systems we put in place and you may want to consider. These include not only information about clients, but also ways to locate documents easier and keep track of the client information the bar association requires you to keep for a long, long time.

- When you first start practicing, everything will be new, so in the beginning things will be a little awkward. Technology has made the practice of law more efficient. And yet – without a process – it is still a daunting endeavor.

- Computer systems will continue to get faster, with bigger applications (and smaller shapes). But the computer is supposed to be a tool to make life a little easier, rather than something you should spend every other day trying to adapt to. Take the time to write down your processes and procedures. Use technology to automate them, but within parameters that you can monitor and adjust if necessary. If you don't, you'll be doing yourself and your colleagues a great disservice.

- As you get more and more busy, it will be next to impossible to keep track of every case you are working on. Your brain can hold just so much information. To avoid waking up at 3 a.m. wondering whether the client signed a form, a deadline was met, or work needs to get done before a tax or court deadline, creating a worksheet will save you many sleepless nights – the Appendix names most of the ones you will need.

- The more cases you work on, the more difficult it will be for you to do everything, and the more pressure you will be under. Learn how to delegate the things you don't do well, and have a procedure that allows you to easily review and assign projects to your trusted team so that the work gets done efficiently, correctly and on a timely basis.

- We modify our procedures as things change or improve, and we try to keep the team on the same page. One example from real estate: It can be very tedious and time-consuming to create all the paperwork necessary for a seamless closing. However, with a procedure that makes the most of available technology, those standard forms can be automated to complete the process in a fraction of the time. This allows you to maximize your time and bill out at a profitable rate whether you are charging by the hour or on a flat-fee basis.

- Anything you can think of that will be useful to you and your practice should be included. Having said that, don't "over-think" it. Don't wait until you have the perfect CRM to open your doors or get your first client. It doesn't work that way. When you get your first client, you will jump for joy – and then figure out how to actually deliver on what you promised!

What a fine segue into the next section!

CHAPTER 8
THE "WHY" OF OUR WORK: CLIENTS!

In starting the practice, I wanted to be different from other law firms. If you have left a large set-up to strike out on your own, I am sure you also have at least one principle or passion that will govern your enterprise. And it's probably the sort of motivational driver that does not emerge from a DiSC analysis or the Kolbe tests.

You might even need a week alone in a national forest – not to get a feel for the core point, which is already known or at least "felt," but to really think through its implications for the next several years.

As the client's trusted advisor, you are in a unique position to find out what makes him or her tick. More than just knowing the law, you need to know that person, that family. You have to become someone the client will turn to, even for problems you can't solve. Knowing who to connect them with will earn many "merit badges" in the relationship game.

A colleague of mine recounted a discussion with his father, also a lawyer, about what a lawyer does. The father's contribution was: "Lawyers solve problems for which their clients lack either the knowledge or the courage to solve themselves." He added: "It is in the second category that we earn our bread."

I really liked the way he put that. And I intended to create long-term relationships with clients, be a resource they could turn to in a time of need, and address the issues that impacted them most. That approach differed mightily from being a technician called in to simply certify processes and appear now and then in court.

The warnings came in: Without real-estate closings and litigation, I was told, the practice wouldn't thrive and might not even survive. But I was persistent and eventually created a successful practice centered on long-term relationships. We were busy and prosperous.

And yet – something was missing. With certain exceptions, I didn't feel I was addressing the clients' needs deep down. At such times – our religious friends refer to it as "a crisis of the faith" – it is good to go back to family members, high-school buddies, or the experienced mentor who has been a wise focuser when fog is getting the better of you.

And, if you are fortunate, a source of guidance

might come to you seemingly out of nowhere. In this case it appeared in the office mail – a big, bulky package arrived. While cleaning out her basement, my stepsister had come across a whole bunch of paperwork from my father.

Dad was fun-loving at home and well-liked by his peers – but a perfectionist in every way, and something of a stoic. He was very determined, very methodical, and the one person we all could turn to in a time of need. When you had a problem, you would bring it to Dad and he would solve your problem. (You might not like his answer, but it would solve the problem!)

As I read through the paperwork – and saw his draft card and his discharge papers from the army during World War II – I encountered a handwritten letter my dad sent to his dad, my grandfather. Dad used to work in my grandfather's restaurant in New York and, in those days, it was hard work.

The letter began this way: "My dear Papa, I can no longer live at home. We fight too much. This is the hardest letter I've ever had to write." The letter went on and on; and, as I was reading it, I was crying my eyes out.

Upon finishing the letter, I recognized that it changed my perception of my Dad. From the image of a stoic, hard, determined individual, he became a very sensitive man who had difficulty expressing himself in a tender way. I always knew that he loved me, and also realized he usually had difficulty expressing it.

And that's when it happened: At that very moment, I recognized that he had missed out on a golden opportunity. He had never been asked the question: "If you had the opportunity to share your wisdom, hopes and dreams with your son or daughter, what would you tell them?" It struck me that this was the treasure that was missing from my own practice.

So I started asking my clients those types of Legacy questions – ones that create a lasting testimonial to the generations of Wealth-Creators. As I talk to people about creating their Ultimate Legacies, I see tears well up in their eyes, and they find it to be the most moving and amazing service we offer.

When we start talking to clients about what success means to them, or what life was like when growing up, or their memories about a special person or child in their lives, their eyes light up. You can see the emotion that makes them who they are today. And it makes the practice so much more rewarding.

It gives clients a testimonial that they're passionate about, which they can easily share with their families or organizations.

The amazing result is that it is changing lives and the way we practice. The conversations are astounding and moving both for my clients and myself.

I recognized that I would give anything to read the wisdom my father would have shared with my brother and me. Now I can give that gift to my clients. Through that humble beginning and my association with various other pioneers in the field, I started sharing that realization with my clients. We now have processes that record our Ultimate Legacy discussions for clients to take and share with their families or organizations. In addition, we have implemented technologies that allow us to actually incorporate their own words into the legal documents without destroying the validity of those documents.

More on that – the principles and behaviors of what I call a Purposeful Law Firm – after we plow through a few more of the management and marketing realms...

CHAPTER 9
ACCOUNTING, PAYROLL AND TAXES

This chapter is about working on the business rather than working in the business. "Accounting, taxes and payroll" might sound mundane, but they are no more mundane than eyesight, blood-circulation and your spinal cord – when any of these factors go down, we then appreciate what was keeping them afloat.

To make sure the firm is meeting its goals, you need to know how your practice is doing, on at least a monthly basis. In our firm, we have a meeting every Monday where we review the status of each current case along with several prospective cases. This kind of meeting helps organize the cash flow, keeps you in sync with most of what's going on in the office, and helps you manage the cases and assign various tasks to the team.

That every-Monday discussion also helps to make sure nothing falls through the cracks. As you get busier, you will find it harder to remember everything that needs to be done, especially if you have a deadline-driven practice like tax or litigation.

In addition, it will help you sleep at night knowing that you and your team have a handle on everything and how each matter is progressing.

I would recommend that you balance the firm's checkbook every month and prepare financial statements (or, at the very least, review profit and loss) so you can see what you have done month-by-month and plan for the next month. Once you have been practicing for a few months and get a feel for actual expenses, you should create a monthly budget detailing income and expenses to keep your spending on track. It's a great way to stay focused and determine where you are going rather than waiting until the end of the year.

And, as a way to stay current on taxes, it helps to determine what your personal income tax liability will be at the end of the year or for your quarterly estimates.

Another sound practice is to hire a service to prepare the payroll. In our office, everyone gets a salary and the payroll company does a great job of preparing the bi-monthly payroll and withholding the taxes. You never want to get behind in paying taxes, especially for employees and their withholdings.

In the early years, money is likely be tight and the tendency is to focus on making the next payroll, cover the rent, and pay for most anything else before taking care of the IRS. Two words: BIG MISTAKE. The cost for neglecting withholding and the payroll tax obligation is a stiff 100% penalty – plus, the IRS can slap a levy on your bank account to get paid. Make sure the IRS gets paid, on time.

Your other creditors also like to get paid on a regular basis. If things are tight, you might be tempted to dodge phone calls from creditors reminding you that their bill is past due. Don't avoid, engage. If you talk to your creditors and explain that you are expecting a check in a couple of weeks, they will work with you. Evading your creditors makes them assume you don't want to pay them. Besides, you will rest easier if you've been up-front with them.

A great friend and client explained to me his firm's way of staying on track. At the end of the month after bills were paid, they would set aside enough money to cover next month's payroll and rent. The balance left after paying bills and set-asides was divided between the partners. Your team (and you) will appreciate that the payroll gets paid first, which will keep them happy and working hard.

I get a salary of a modest amount and – given that the LLC is taxed as an S Corporation – the net profit at the end of the year is taxable to me on my individual return. Making sure that you are aware of the tax liability and keeping track of it monthly is key.

Should you hire a bookkeeper or accountant? If you have a tax background, great – but, as the practice gets busier, you may not have time to devote to tracking the financials. I prefer to do monthly accountings and bank reconciliations; but, if that would be a chore for you, nothing is wrong with having a bookkeeper come in a couple of times a month. It will also open up that time so you can do more to raise revenues for the firm.

I used to prepare my own LLC and individual tax forms, but it became time- consuming and something of a distraction. Throw in the fact that – even though I am a CPA as well as an attorney and have prepared hundreds of tax returns in my career – a good accountant is worth every penny to make sure you are on track with the IRS and the returns are prepared correctly.

You should seek out a CPA who not only prepares returns, but can counsel you on better ways to get those important tax-deductions. They may even spot items that you might not be aware of, potentially saving you even more tax dollars.

CHAPTER 10
HIRING AND MANAGING LAWYERS

You may have heard that many lawyers are looking for jobs. That's true, but many have been downsized from larger firms and may retain expectations about workload and salary that exceed your ability to pay.

In my experience, younger lawyers have high expectations that might not be justified by their levels of experience and education. Other lawyers – those who graduated from top schools or were at the top of their class – are likely to be scooped up by the big firms and won't have to alter their lofty expectations.

Another point to keep in mind – if you hire a lawyer, especially a younger one, recognize that they might stay a few years and then, typically after some disagreement with you, strike out on their own taking some of your clients with them. To reduce this risk, it is important to have employees sign a non-compete, non-disclosure and confidentiality agreement.

I used the phrase "taking some of your clients..."

It's easy to be informal with that kind of talk. Of course, the clients are not "your" clients. The clients are free to choose whatever lawyer they want, and for that matter, to download their forms from LegalZoom.com. If the lawyer you hired was the primary point of contact with the client, meanwhile you haven't really taken the time to get to know that client, they will likely go with the lawyer that has built their trust – which in this case will not be you.

So, even though you'll want to delegate the workload to other team members, you also need to stay involved and touch base with the client often enough. Neither control freak nor egomaniac, you trust the people under you to help get the work done on a timely basis, but always remember it is easier to keep an existing client than try to find a new one. They are looking to you for help in times of need. Make sure you nurture each client relationship.

Many factors influence whether you hire an experienced lawyer or one who is relatively inexperienced but arrives with offsetting positives. Do you need to have someone "hit the ground running" so that you can delegate to them right away? Or are you willing to train them – adapt this new person to your style and the firm's culture – so that they execute the processes you have developed in a consistent manner?

Someone right out of law school can probably be groomed to your standards. Many factors will influence this decision. For example, for someone who has never worked in an office, you may need to instruct them how to properly present themselves as a lawyer, both in writing and in office etiquette. Or they may require training in Microsoft Office or other necessary technologies (See Chapter 6). This will be more challenging and time-consuming than simply hiring someone with pre-packaged skills, but it could also have big payoff by the second or third year.

Having said that, there may be other reasons – intangible factors – that make it wise to hire a particular person. This is something that you feel in your gut. For example, the person you are considering might have a great work ethic or a lot of drive, and these qualities can offset their lack of experience.

Choosing team members will not be easy and you may want to consider using an outside service to help screen and find qualified candidates. At least aim to have someone you trust – someone who understands your employee requirements and office culture – take part in the interviewing process.

When our practice had reached the point where another lawyer was needed to help with the workload, I hired an outside company to assist with the hiring process. I had tried to do it on my own for other team members in the past, and seemed to pick the wrong people for each job that needed filling. I wanted a long-term, career-minded person to fill the lawyer position. I wanted someone with a little experience but, because we are a small firm, I could not compete salary-wise with the large downtown firms.

All in all, there were many constraints on hiring this new person.

How to proceed? With the help of the outside firm, we built an interview schedule and developed a standard list of questions that we could ask each of the candidates to consistently measure their responses. Then the outsourcing company put ads in the paper, screened out the "bad" applicants or those who didn't fit and selected three of the best applicants for the job. It made the process more efficient, and even though I had to pay the outsourcing firm a fee, the investment was well worth it in terms of time saved and the lawyer we eventually hired.

We ended up with an excellent lawyer, not only

with a strong grasp of estate planning, but also as an excellent legal draftsman. It got to the point that I could delegate any assignment to him and he would take care of it effectively and efficiently.

When he first started, I set down lofty goals with timelines for completing the related tasks. We also scheduled time on the calendar for a mini-review after three, six and nine months to make sure the goals were still appropriate and to evaluate progress. Don't imagine you can hire someone, assign work and assume it will get done in a timely fashion. Create goals for them to accomplish within time-lines and deadlines. And give them feedback periodically so you can "course-correct" as you go.

Here's the first criterion we apply to any associate or new employee: "Is there a fit between the associate/employee and our firm?" An individual's goals and intensity change as he or she becomes more complacent in his or her role, so you need to constantly reassess whether your employee has the drive and ambition to advance the culture and goals of the firm. This person could be a future partner, your greatest confidante, or even an "heir apparent," so you want to keep on top of the work they are doing and the progress they are making.

Continuing with the main story: In just a year,

my associate had received several increases in salary and was working quite well – to the point that I could now help to expand his skill set. We both recognized that though he was an excellent in-house lawyer, he lacked the desire to market and bring in business. He felt that I was the rainmaker and he was – this is my term, not his – a "worker bee." I suggested to him that, while he did very good work, the time had come for him to demonstrate commitment to the firm by going out into the community and generating new business.

What happened next was a surprise. He told me he didn't want to go that route and that his commitment was to simply do his work every day. Arriving at around 8:15 and leaving promptly at 5:00, he worked hard and accomplished much. But he wasn't interested in marketing, or going to seminars, or to bar and other professional meetings after 5 pm. That was not a good relationship, long-term, for the firm, so we mutually decided to part company.

Did I do the right thing? You might have handled it differently, based on your firm's culture and near-term needs. That's fine. I was probably especially demanding because, after all, he was the first lawyer to be hired in my firm. And if he were allowed to evade the "everybody is a marketer" principle, the policy would be very hard to maintain with anyone else in the future. You might someday welcome a purely in-house legal whiz who, for whatever reason, insists on fixed hours. No part of my tale is locked in stone, except for this part: Be clear about your expectations for new hires, especially during the first critical year.

The next person hired, also through the outside firm, was a little more experienced, with an LLM in taxation (actually there were two candidates that were pretty good). But I later found out that though they believed they were up to the task, they lacked the experience and expertise needed for the day-to-day work. They had great resumes, but didn't have the actual experience of working with clients every day and dealing with the unexpected.

The gentleman I eventually hired was marketing-oriented, and he asked me what he would get if he brought in a client. His drive was commendable, but his timing and tone were terrible. I explained to him that he had only been with us three weeks and if he brought in a client (which after all was part of his responsibilities), it would be a plus when bonus and raise-time came.

That was all fine, he replied, but if he referred

the case to another firm, they would give him a referral fee. Yes, and what of it? Well, he continued – remember, this conversation is taking place during our first month – he expected at least the same referral fee from me!

What would you have said? I replied that he was an employee of the firm, and any clients he brought in would be our firm's clients unless and until he became a partner and had bought into the firm. To make a long story short, he lasted about three months.

If you want them to bring in business for the firm – maybe not during the first six months, but soon enough – how are you going to reward them? And then – can you proceed in that manner without negatively affecting or simply confusing your other employees?

More generally, when it comes to hiring lawyers: Choose wisely, choose slowly, and keep conversing, revising your perspective, and tracking your new colleague's performance. Don't let the workload dictate a quick hire, and make sure you keep in mind the type of person you want to hire in light of the team dynamics. What will truly be needed from this new hire?

CHAPTER 11
MORE NETWORKING:
COLLABORATING IN PUBLIC

After working in the practice (not "on" the practice) for several years, I had the good fortune to meet a colleague who was having great success giving Living Trust seminars. He became very busy very quickly by working with financial advisors and putting on seminars to explain the benefits of Living Trusts.

This individual was a very talented teacher and mentor – instantly, people would like and trust him. He was, and still is, a brilliant estate-planning lawyer, in addition to being highly innovative. So he and I began working together in ways that produced some very effective seminars.

My partner was working very hard, and the practice was successful. After finding that running his practice day-to-day had become a drain on his energy, he looked to make a change. After some discussion about our individual goals, we arranged for me to buy the practice.

Not surprisingly, I kept up the same method – seminars – to bring in business. About 50% of our attendees would become clients. Unfortunately, the number of people who were attending began to dwindle. My associates and I were putting in more and more effort only to wind up with a static or slipping participation rate. If we didn't do something differently, there wouldn't be a practice in the not-too-distant future.

Please don't misunderstand why this story is here. Seminars remain one of the best ways to get your name out there and attract new business. After all, you are educating people. You are serving them, using proven ideas and methods. And they're already a customer – because they invested an hour or a day – which is halfway to becoming a client.

However, my experience is that people, in the Chicago area if not everywhere else, are "seminared out." Unless the subject matter and level of interaction are enough to grab their interest, it will be difficult to sustain a practice based solely on seminar marketing.

And so, if you intend to make that kind of bet – to make or keep seminars as your primary draw for new business – try to connect with a financial professional or CPA who has a similar outlook on marketing. You can then jointly plan to put on seminars. This way you can share the costs, expand the content offered to participants, and maximize the ROI.

Better yet, if you can secure a speaking engagement from an organization that will bring a group of people to the meeting, the burden on you to find attendees is eliminated. You will also quickly become a subject-matter expert, especially to the participants.

So if you decide to include seminars as part of your marketing mix, begin by evaluating who is in your target audience and what they would be interested in learning. Determine the demographic you are trying to reach – individuals, retirees, business-owners, age range and income, or size of estates – and search for the organizations or groups in which that demographic congregates.

Some time ago, I was working with the regional manager of a major property and casualty insurance company. These are great contacts to have with because they usually have many of the clients you want to work with and most of those clients have not done the foundational work they need to do.

First, we arranged for me to put on a seminar for all the agents detailing ways we could work together, the benefits to their clients, and the benefit to the agents themselves. Though agents had focused most of their time on selling property and casualty insurance, they were also licensed to sell life insurance. The company was making a major push to encourage its agents to sell life insurance to their existing clients, but they had a hard time making that a reality. The company realized that the agents could make far more in commissions by selling life insurance; and yet many of them – already making a very good living with P&C – didn't feel motivated to try something new.

By educating this group of advisors, we created a way to help solve their existing clients' needs, and increase their income without having to find a new client. We also put on seminars for their business clients. The result was a win-win-win for everyone – clients, advisors and us.

You may want to find the kinds of advisors in your area who have some synergy with your practice and actively market together.

Find the topic that works in your area and connect with people who can get you in front of your potential client base.

Here's another example: People might not want to come to a Living Trust seminar, but they might be more interested in a seminar on how to maximize and protect your retirement savings or how to increase profits. Business owners are a difficult group to reach, but if you plan something in the morning with a light breakfast, promise they won't be sold anything and will be out by 9 a.m., the right topic can draw the crowd you're looking for. (Something like: "The five things that keep business owners awake at night and how to avoid them.")

Be creative and make use of input from advisors, clients and business owners you trust. Join with one of your trusted advisors to create a focus group or poll their clients as to what they might be interested in and then create a program or marketing strategy around that topic.

Last point: Be wary of claims by people who offer to help you set up seminars. In my experience, many of them have had success in the region they are located (California or Florida, for example) but that performance might not carry over easily or effectively to a different geographical area.

CHAPTER 12
ESTATE PLANNING FOR ULTIMATE LEGACIES

Many people experience fear when they hear "estate planning" and "succession planning." The more direct term, and the one this book leans toward, is exit planning. But, whatever the term, the prospect of it seems to give people the jitters. They would rather not discuss it.

Some people might cover it by simply signing documents to put in a drawer. Or they assume they can "get by," and save some money using very simple documents. Doing so misses the bigger picture – the impact on the family from the transfer of wealth. Will it be carried out consciously or haphazardly? Is the objective to do right by two or more generations, along with the one who hasn't arrived yet, or simply to limit what the IRS can claim?

Until you sit with a client and find out some information about their family, values and goals, you will not know what they have at risk or how to help. You need to counsel the client and explain to him or her the "sleeper" issues, give them new options, and help them clarify the best course of action.

Early in 2014, I received a call from an advisor who was trying to retain a client for insurance planning. (The facts have been changed slightly to protect client confidentiality, but this tale illustrates the critical point.) The client is a very successful seller of office products. He was very concerned about the operation of the business, getting the next big deal, and covering his payroll every week.

So we engaged in a conversation to learn more about what his goals were and how we might help. What did we learn? The estate was large enough to be taxable, the day-to-day operations are run by family members, and three very competitive sons work in the business.

I asked him, "Who is the best one to run the business?" He responded: "My oldest son, Brad." He also indicated that while he had a good relationship with his sons, most family gatherings were like business meetings rather than father-son chats. I asked how the business was structured – corporation or LLC – and who owned the business interests. He replied: "My wife owns all the interests as it's a woman-owned business." He also indicated that she didn't work actively in the business and really didn't know too much about its operations.

Even the most down-to-earth business, and one where all the key players talk to each other every day, can work itself into some amazingly complex ruts.

The scenario deserved clarification: "Just so I understand – if you were to pass away tomorrow, your expectation is that your wife will choose one of your very competitive sons to run the business and keep the family cash flow healthy; is that right?" He nodded his head. I then asked: "How, in practice, do you think that is going to work?"

The emotional context for this type of future is rarely anticipated, which means the client has to be helped to see that this and similar situations are fraught with danger – to the point they could possibly split up the family as well as ruin a business.

A principle concept of estate planning and contract law is that the Trust-Creator's intent and directions, as expressed in the documents, should control future decisions and their wishes in other matters should generally be adhered to. But, as technology has changed and wealth has been accumulated, we are being asked more and more to create documents and plans that could endure for generations.

So how does even a thoughtful law firm

anticipate what could happen 100 years after the Trust-Creator has died? Or how the family's needs are evolving?

For the readers who are old enough to remember Alan Shepard, the first American in space, I'll share this scene: I was a young boy at the time, but I remember being brought with my class into the auditorium so we could watch the launch on TV. What an awesome event. None of us watching could have even fathomed that a tiny box in your pocket could function as a smartphone and carry as much computing power as a mainframe computer did 30 years ago. The point is that we cannot anticipate that which we do not know, especially aspects that aren't yet part of our mainstream of life.

That's why we need to create plans that are flexible enough to accommodate those changes that will invariably occur. Sometimes that means giving the Trustee the discretion to make decisions based on his or her assessment of the situation at the time. Remember, your client won't be there, so their hand-picked successor will have to make judgment calls on their behalf.

Furthermore, when control or direction of a business is involved, especially a family business that the founder would like to see pass from generation to generation, having a vision statement or "constitution" makes some sense. Why not put down the owner-founder's vision so that later generations of family know what the original intent was? Why not allow the document to accommodate changes that will occur in the future even though their specifics can't be predicted or scripted?

A good design will let a governing board, composed of family members and valued outsiders or trusted key employees, guide the transition of the business over time. This can eliminate or forestall a whole host of problems and disharmony.

Traditionally, the documents that we have drafted were not meant to be changed after someone passed away. But two relatively new concepts in estate planning have become very helpful.

1. TRUST-PROTECTORS.

These individuals are named in trust documents to effectively protect the trust that is being created. Typically, they are not trustees and, if they seek to carry out both roles, they'll encounter problems coming and going.

This section is not a treatise on Trust-Protectors, but essentially they act in several very important functions. They can hire and fire trustees if succession is not named or if the appointed trustee is not performing their job correctly.

This is especially important if an institution is named as trustee and the institution changes over time. Right before and especially during the 'Crash of 2008,' many smaller banks were taken over by larger banks. The client liked working with the trust officer at ABC Bank and Trust; but, when the bank's ownership shifted, that person was replaced. The Trust-Protector can help in that sort of situation.

Also, if there is a change in the tax law or a "scrivener's error" (a typo) that alters the Trust-Creator's intent, the Trust-Protector can – of course with the approval of the current beneficiaries – change the trust without the expense of going to court for reformation. A useful tool to keep in mind, but be wary of its application: You will act in a fiduciary capacity if you accept this role. These rules are very complex and may vary from state to state, so be sure to check your state statutes if you use them.

2. DECANTING.

As in decanting wine, we "pour" the trust from one "bottle" to another, more appropriate "bottle" to accomplish the Trust-Creator's intent. Again, a matter more complex than can be handled in a book like this one. Just know that Decanting is useful to have in your tool kit to adapt to changing conditions especially if you create trusts that are meant to last for decades.

Some states, like Illinois, have passed legislation outlining Trust-Protector's duties and Decanting prerequisites; if your state has those statues, you may want to familiarize yourself with the duties, rights and obligations under them.

Some readers, though, are already there. And this is the moment in the book where I hope to speak to lawyers who are young and restless – or who, say at age 50, are restless in part because they are no longer young!

Chapter Eight referred to a shock of recognition upon knowing that my father had never been given the chance to answer some form of this question: "If you had the opportunity to share your wisdom, hopes and dreams with your son or daughter, what would you tell them?" And the epiphany I had in realizing that the real treasures were the stories that explained clients' values – the values that they wanted to share and pass on to their children.

That is the real inheritance that became the "treasure" to be worked into my own practice – the thing to help client-families "discover" and capture.

More so than tactics and tools, the Ultimate Legacy conversations are astounding and moving. They sometimes bring about emotional struggle for clients, but you can learn so much about the families you deal with by bringing them closer together and creating a much deeper relationship. These transformative client-family discussions enhance their lives, and in the process your own practice is enhanced.

I would have given anything to read my father's shared wisdom when I could still discuss it with him. Now I can help my clients capture that gift to share with their loved ones.

Seeking out pioneers in the field, I started sharing that wisdom with my clients. It took a couple of years, but now it's quite practical for us to record Ultimate Legacy conversations to preserve these treasured stories, enabling clients to share them with families or values-based organizations. The technology that allows us to incorporate our clients' actual words, without destroying the documents' validity, allows us to transform ordinarily dry legal documents so that they come alive for the Trust-Creators who add their stories and wisdom to them.

As with other advanced offerings, the people who would most welcome such services don't necessarily know that they exist. Most people don't come in expecting our type of Legacy conversation, though we are happy to help those who are content to put the documents in a drawer and forget about it. Others who show some curiosity are offered three ways to do what my father never did:

Option #1: We sit down with clients, record a 30-minute conversation, and cover the things – beliefs, principles, goals – that are important to them and their loved ones. In 30 minutes, with no trouble or fuss, we can shape a treasure for their loved ones that they will cherish as I do my dad's papers.

Option #2: We have the capability to put a clients' words into the estate plan documents so that their voice – the wisdom or life lessons they want to impart – is part of the trust. Every time the trustee makes a distribution from the trust, the beneficiary will know the client's intent behind it.

Option #3: We can help clients keep the

family harmonious by opening a dialogue about their shared legacy and vision allowing their Ultimate Legacy to benefit future generations. Rather than leaving their family feeling empty, they can leave their family with successful and fulfilled lives. We can create a safe place to learn about money and what Legacy means, thereby creating successful life stories. We can help clients arrange their affairs so that loved ones can benefit, while still preserving the family fortune.

Through such meetings, family members can learn life's lessons, but in a setting that emphasizes learning these lessons together, and focusing on what can be accomplished as a whole. We find these conversations to be extremely valuable for both our clients and us.

On one occasion, I was talking to a client who had a fairly thick accent, and I said to him in the course of our interview, "You were obviously not raised in Chicago. Tell me about what it was like where you grew up." The man reflected a moment, then a big smile crossed his face.

He started to relate a story about the old fishing hole back home, where his father taught him how to fish and how they would spend hours and hours, talking, sometimes fishing and always laughing. He remembered how close he, his father, and his brother were during those days, and I could tell by the look in his eyes, that he was reliving those days as if they were yesterday. He related many stories that morning, and I was fascinated. To this day, he and I are closer than ever.

On another occasion, I had gone to visit a new client who lived alone in an independent-living situation. As she welcomed me into her home, I was struck by the order with which she kept her home – everything in its place. To her, her home was a thing of pride, and you could tell her whole life had been just as orderly.

She was delighted to have a visitor, and as she showed me her beautiful condo, I noticed pictures of a gentleman throughout the house. I asked if they were pictures of her husband. She said yes and related that he had died about a year ago, and that they had been married for over 60 years.

Madge (not her real name) was about 80 at the time and as she stared at the picture she started to remember. It was a picture of her husband, taken during World War II, and they had met and married fairly quickly, as many did at the time. She told me that they had a wonderful relationship, and started a family when he returned.

We spent the next two hours sharing stories (okay, she shared, I listened). What a wonderful gift I was given that day and we each found a new friend. That friendship continues to this day, and my team and I always look forward to meetings with her because they are so enriching.

This transformation helped us create systems and processes that help families connect with a group of caring advisors who understand each family's vision, and who work to create Ultimate Legacies that will last for generations. By engaging in these conversations, I saw client relationships becoming stronger and more meaningful, both for the clients and ourselves. They now look to us as their trusted advisor, not only for estate planning, but they also seek our counsel for referrals to others who have an expertise outside of our own.

The point here is that by engaging in some client outreach that goes beyond simply expressing your expertise, you will establish relationships with not only clients, but also potential referral sources. They will see that you are the type of lawyer, the type of person with whom they want to deal.

Furthermore, we were able to develop a way to

blend legal expertise, authentic client connection, and proven wealth protection strategies to help people prepare for tomorrow with customized estate, business and asset protection plans, and you can develop a similar strategy that works for you and your clients.

For some people, successful planning may mean a simple will and regular payments into an IRA. For others, it may mean a wealth-replacement trust, a family limited-liability company, or a complicated business-exit strategy.

Our services include:

- Business counseling, succession and exit planning
- Estate planning
- Trusts and trust administration
- Wills
- Probate assistance
- Educational seminars

I would suggest you need to have a message that clients can hold onto and really express what you do to others. This will get the word-of-mouth "buzz" going and establish you not only as the expert in your field of endeavor, but people will be drawn to you, refer you and engage you as a client.

CHAPTER 13
MOVING FROM PRAGMATIC TO PURPOSEFUL

Many great people have shown me how to run the Stuart Legacy Alliance in a manner that makes working here enjoyable. But two stand out for the way they have changed the nature and focus of our practice.

I have much admiration, and give many thanks, for the brilliant work of John A. Warnick and Scott Farnsworth. In their own ways, each taught me different methods of making the practice meaningful and establishing deeper and more trusting relationships with the clients and advisors with whom we interact.

Scott is founder of the Sunbridge Network which enables professionals and other advisors to capture and promote intergenerational legacies and stories. He is committed to estate plans that will profoundly affect their heirs and reflect their value. Scott is an excellent attorney who sees the connection between creating meaningful trusts and integrating clients' values into their estate plans. He has taught me the merit of conveying stories as a tool, creating deeper relationships with clients, and he helped me better understand the values that keep families together. To find out more about Scott and the Sunbridge Network, I urge you to visit their website at www.sunbridgelegacy.com

Running an estate planning practice requires not only that you are technically competent, but also that you understand what makes your clients and their families tick. We have to understand the dynamics of a family to be able to help them in their moments of need. To do so, we must delve into the emotional issues, dig deeper to get to know them, and then center on what they want to accomplish through the planning process.

After all, many of the trusts we create are meant to last for several generations. How can this be accomplished without knowing the Trust-Creator's intent? It can't! I had a sense of this "gap" years ago. That's why I always wanted the ability to include some such statement of intent in the documents. The problem is that various colleagues told me that doing so would destroy the legal structure and harm the court validity of the documents.

That dilemma and others begin to dissolve after I met John A. Warnick, founder of the Purposeful Planning Institute and creator of the Purposeful

Planning "Collaboratory." John A. (which is how he likes to be known) is a brilliant and creative lawyer who feels the same way, and who pioneered a technology that allows you to counsel with clients and include their intent in the documents without destroying the legalese.

If you are interested in finding out more about "PPI," I encourage you to visit www.PurposefulPlanningInstitute.com. Pay special attention to the section listing the regional workshops that he puts on – there are several each year.

The idea behind PPI, and especially its annual mid-summer Rendezvous, is to create a group of advisors with a variety of backgrounds to enhance a particular client relationship and, more importantly, to create the best result for that client.

Accountants, lawyers, wealth managers, counselors (both business and personal), coaches and others all work together collaboratively for a given family.

Sometimes the collaboration lasts for a year or more; other times, three different professionals will zero in on one set of tough issues for a few days. When the varied professionals have the same "purposeful" mindset, this approach can move mountains and plant the seeds of multi-generational forests.

To help clients in need, I have worked with many professionals from the Collaboratory – including estate planners who have a slightly different focus on the type of work that they do.

For example, if I am doing exit planning for a business client and they need a business coach to help them navigate the waters of disagreeing partners, or if they need help setting up a management team to keep the business running in the event the founder can't, I can call on one of my colleagues to help smooth that process.

On one occasion recently, I received a call from a financial advisor who was trying to retain a client. The latter has a small but well-known business in the northern suburbs around Chicago. Some 75 years ago, the grandfather of the current owners came to this country and started the business.

As the advisor explained it, two current owners each controlled 50% of the business; they are brothers and, for one reason or another, could not see eye to eye. (Not an atypical situation. In fact, I sometimes think the psychologists who explore "sibling rivalry" ought to be writing business manuals.)

My friend asked if I would join him in the meeting with this prospect and explain to them the collaborative dimension of our practices. On the way there, we knew there might be some resistance to having more than one professional counseling them. So we explained that we each had different areas of expertise, and outlined the need they had for both.

As many prospects do, they indicated that they had current counsel and really didn't need to add to those services and costs. Of course, that meant doing something, on the spot, to see how urgent their need was.

The two owners realized that they were at an impasse, the board was deadlocked, and that if something wasn't done soon, the business would fall apart – and they would have nothing to pass to the fourth generation. After a brief discussion of these bottom-line realities, it became clear to all of us that, although their current advisors were good in their specific niches, they were not up to speed on the type of consulting this critical situation called for.

We were able to bring together a collaborative group of four advisors – myself as the estate and business attorney; a management consultant; a CPA; and a business psychologist – each one well-versed in business dynamics and succession or exit planning. Here's the amazing truth: The perspective that each of us brought to the planning process was critical to its success. The result was stronger planning, and the client is better off for it today.

In this particular situation, the business psychologist (or business coach) was instrumental in getting the two family members and 50/50 shareholders on board with a plan to move forward. I think this would have been very difficult had he – the psychologist – not been a part of the process. He would generally do more listening than speaking. And, when he spoke up to raise issues, they were right on point; this psychologist was able to defuse potential explosions while making certain compromises easier for all to absorb.

To say the least, working collaboratively makes the process function better, makes the planning stronger, and gets the client to the point they need to get to – with far less grief and fog than if one advisor tried to go it alone.

If I might state it more plainly: When one advisor indicates to a client that they can do everything, especially in an exit planning meeting with a business owner, I think they are not being truthful to themselves or with the client.

By working in a collaborative manner, the team recognizes where issues arise and allows for the appropriate team member to address the areas relating to their expertise. The result is that the client receives better and more effective counseling to reach their goals. This adds perceptible value to the process – and, quite frankly, it increases your value to the client.

When this is done sincerely, and with no hidden agenda, it will pay great dividends.

We have created a group of individuals to whom we regularly turn when there is an issue we grapple with. And the members of our Succession Collaboratory will help when they can and are committed to doing a great job for the client as their first priority.

John A. Warnick has a philosophy that an "attitude of gratitude" goes a long way to bonding with people, and clients in particular. He is a pioneer and is creating a groundswell of enthusiasm for this kind of planning. Call it a "movement" if you like but, in my view, given public opinion about the reputation of lawyers, fresh approaches like this one are essential.

By understanding the clients' mission, vision, values, and goals, you can work more effectively on their behalf and they will be grateful for it. John A. has created the framework. And the more his friends and allies can advance that framework, the better off the general public – and especially high-net-worth families and multi-generation businesses – will be.

CHAPTER 14
MAKING THE PRACTICE (EVEN)
MORE PURPOSEFUL

"Be different in some meaningful way and stand out from the crowd." So we are told by nearly all the marketing experts. And I am not here to disagree.

In order to prosper over time, lawyers and law firms need to avoid falling into the rut of "commoditization." Commoditization means that your product or service is fungible and not greatly different from anyone else's. If that's the case, you will end up competing based on price.

The larger firms are trying to differentiate themselves based on name recognition. Perhaps the larger corporations will keep hiring the big-name law firms – given that "big" seems to feel more comfortable with other "big" – but we smaller guys and gals out here have far more maneuverability and we ought to use it.

More families realize that certain types of relationships – meaningful, purposeful ones – are unlikely from the big-name firms. These families want value and they are willing to pay for a purposeful relationship based on that value.

Such a demand brings forth new suppliers – which is much easier to see when watching American retailers. Whoever thought that buying a cup of coffee would cost us $4.00? Clients are more educated and want an experience, as opposed to a transaction or a one-shot consultation. (And, from Starbucks, they can purchase a "double-shot" at the low price of $2.69.) Your law firm, whether new or long-standing, must stand out in some way; and your clients must value that distinctiveness if you are to have a healthy enterprise.

Creating a purposeful law practice – one geared to more than accumulating tax deductions and passing money and property to the next generation – is the most exciting and effective path open to you. You'll be addressing a way of communicating from generation to generation – something of real value, coming from the heart of the Trust-Creator – that families will appreciate decades from now.

How many times have you heard about a later generation – "G2" or "G3" – being ruined because they received an inheritance? If the Trust-Creators set down what the inheritance will mean, and what the successor generation(s) can accomplish or advance, the risks of family decay and disillusion go way down. When the meaning or aspirations behind the money and property – the wealth set to pass from one generation to the next – is known and shared, future generations will be better served.

I will close this section – though the book has more to go – with one of my favorite stories from the Warnick "Seedlings" blog at www.PurposefulPlanningInstitute.com:

The Chinese Meaning of Money

Reprinted with permission

George McDonald observed that "it is by loving and not by being loved that one can come nearest to the soul of another" (George McDonald Anthology, Geoffrey Bles, London, 1970).

Every time I read the words of George McDonald I am reminded of this powerful lesson which a Chinese-American friend of mine shared with me. During lunch one day he surprised me with this question: "Do you mind if I ask you some very personal questions?"

"Not at all," I replied with a growing sense of curiosity over where this turn in the conversation was taking us.

"I've shared with you a little bit of my Chinese heritage and my feelings about the importance of family. But let me ask you a few questions about how you, as an American, view money, gifts and inheritance and then I'd like to contrast that with what I was taught the Chinese view is. So tell me, what does money mean to you?"

I was somewhat disarmed by the question. A number of concepts raced through my mind. "Well," I replied, "it really can mean or represent a lot of different things. For instance, money is a medium of exchange. It is the way I buy goods or services. But it also represents power and status. On the negative or dark side it represents control and dependency. And perhaps at the highest level it means opportunity, stewardship…"

My voice trailed off as I thought of the powerfully positive ways in which I had seen some of my wealthy clients put their money to use.

"That is such an American definition," my friend chuckled gracefully. "Now would you like to learn how the Chinese view the money which they receive as a gift or inheritance?"

"Oh, yes. Please teach me."

"In China, when we receive an inheritance we view it as the life energy of the person who has given us that money or property, whatever it is. It represents all of their love, toil and experiences. In fact, in a way it not only represents the culmination of their life's efforts but it is an extension of the opportunities, successes and sacrifices of all of their ancestors. So when we spend some of our inheritance, it is to us as if we are spending the life energy of our ancestor(s)."

It was in that moment that I first began to understand that there is another meaning to money which could dramatically change the way inheritors and trust beneficiaries regard the wealth they receive. Is there another paradigm around the meaning of money you can share with us?

CHAPTER 15
EASING OUT MEANS THINKING WAY AHEAD

I wrote this book for every lawyer with an independent mindset. Parts of it will be valuable for the man or woman who is 28; and other parts will take longer – requiring more of your time and travails in the profession – to seem practical. (Remember the subtitle that wasn't used: "The life-cycle of a law firm.")

Since we're down to the final two chapters, the most attentive readers are likely to be between the ages of 45 and 60. So let's assume your law business is running well and things are going fine. And the time is approaching when you'll need to transition the firm.

Most attorneys I talk to about transitioning their practice look at me like I'm crazy: "What do you mean 'get out'? I'll work until they carry me out feet-first!" The odds are that nearly everyone who says that – along with some who don't even think it – will end up that way. In point of fact, most lawyers (and for that matter most business-owners) are not thinking about their end game, but rather how to bring in the next big case or meet their payroll obligations next month.

So let's consider: What about the quality of your life at this point in time? Do you really want to continue putting in 90+ hours per week as you have been for the past 30 years?

When I ask people what they want to do when they retire, they generally respond by saying that they know too many people who have retired to go play golf, and who die soon after, due to boredom. But there's a lot of space between doing a "full stop" and making no changes on the way to a feet-first farewell. You have led a vibrant life, will "own" the practice right up to the moment when a new owner is confirmed, and no way will you be a fast fade whose highlight is five days a week on the golf course. That is a phony choice – so simplistic it ends up serving as an excuse to avoid hard thinking.

As this book goes to press, I am 64. Yes, I love doing what I do, and working with the staff that makes it all possible. I get a kick out of helping clients plan their futures for their families' benefit. Why should "retirement" mean leaving all of that behind? Instead, it will mean working 10 to 20 hours a week, making the same or better money, and spending more time rainmaking or doing the other things I enjoy. I'd like to focus on the activities that make my lifestyle fulfilling, such as getting more involved in my church, serving on charitable and professional organization boards to advance their causes, giving back to the community, and not just playing golf, but also riding my bicycle and traveling.

Who knows, I might even start mentoring other lawyers or provide a sounding board for the smaller firms. The point is, the choice is yours. You have the power to decide what you want to do and what will make a difference in your life or community.

In my mind, the best of all worlds would be doing something that gives back to the community, that allows me to use my talents to help where I can, and still have time for my family, friends and some personal pursuits. So the motto is, as a friend of mine says, "Work hard, have fun, make money" – and I will add, "Just don't kill yourself doing it!" Learn to work smarter not harder and make the practice more fun.

At the time of my 62nd birthday, I reflected on the fact that I have fewer years ahead of me than are behind me. I want them to be the best years of my life and have the most fun with the least stress. The question for me has been the same one you might want to ask yourself: How do you achieve that by your fourth decade in the business?

From the beginning, you have to start thinking about how to continually generate money on an annual basis without working 50 to 90 hours per week. Think about the Internet companies who charge an annual or monthly fee for the services that they provide. If you have annual income coming in from one or more sources, it becomes easier to do the everyday things that raise revenue.

This book began by proclaiming the slow but sure death of the traditional way of practicing law and interacting (or not!) with clients. The transactional practice of law – even when it works – can wear you down. Although estate planning has traditionally been approached in a transactional way, we have developed methods to generate an annual income – approaches that not only add value to the practice, but also provide a mechanism to demonstrate tangible value to clients even as they contribute to covering the overhead.

In actuality, this way of practicing essentially provides the means to ease yourself out. Most law practices die when the senior partner dies, and the cause is the absence of a system to create value beyond him or her. Clients have identified with the partner and he or she is the firm.

When you have created value in the practice – as opposed to centering it on one or two individuals at the firm – you create the platform that would be attractive to a younger lawyer who would like to succeed you. Someone who will carry on the vision you started and take care of your clients, continuing the goodwill you created.

In our practice, I strive to use "we," "us," and "our" rather than "I" or "me." Sure, I am the face of the firm and have established relationships with all the clients. But they also know that anyone in the firm can help them if they need it. Granted that legal questions require a response from one of our lawyers, but there are many other inquiries that the team can help with.

I call the firm The Legacy Alliance for two reasons. One, it establishes that we are a legacy planning firm that does business planning as well as estate planning. Two, the firm's name says "I don't do this alone." It calls for a variety of disciplines that all contribute to the well-being of the client. It is the collaborative nature of the practice that not only creates the best planning for the client, but also helps establish you as their trusted advisor to whom they turn when they have needs even beyond your expertise.

Please note that the examples are not here for self-congratulation or to make my officemates proud. Rather, these examples are structural and strategic. Things designed during your second decade, implemented thoroughly during your third, so that they flower during the fourth – this kind of conscious progression is what allows the firm to outlive you while also allowing you to live well when your weekly interaction with it drops by two-thirds to 90%.

Early on, we developed a process to help clients maintain the estate plans we create for them. In doing so, we are helping them ensure their plans receive proper funding, along with updating their plans periodically so they stay current and up-to-date with changes in their families, personal situations and the law.

In addition to drafting state-of-the-art documents, we also help the clients do the funding and help them transfer assets into the trust name. This allows us to contact them every year and find out more about what is going on with them. It makes the relationship stronger. We can find out if there are additional things they need to be aware of to make the plan better and, naturally, it makes it more likely that they will come to us when someone dies.

One of the big drawbacks with traditional estate planning lawyers is their transactional nature. The lawyers see the client to create documents, review and sign them – followed by zero contact for years. Or maybe they do contact the clients, but the client doesn't feel the need to update anything, or their tax or personal situation hasn't changed – and therefore "why go through the time and expense of seeing a lawyer?"

They might not put the question that way to you, but it's there, and you need to make it interesting for them to keep talking and sharing with you. Otherwise, with no relationship having been established beyond this or that transaction, there is much less chance they will go to the lawyer or firm that drafted the documents when someone dies.

By establishing an annual relationship with clients, the retention rate for settlements when a client dies goes up dramatically. About 95% of our clients come back to us – a dramatic percentage! – when there is a death in the family and they want to settle the estate. We are servicing a need that clients have and it keeps the firm going to help them when they need it most. Most clients don't realize the trauma they will go through when they lose a spouse or a parent. And they consistently tell us that they like having someone attentive to their planning who can provide counsel on changes that affect them.

When my dad died, mom had to restructure her whole life to take care of two young kids. I started the firm in part because I felt that no one should have to face that alone. Remember, these were the days when fathers controlled or took care of everything financial. Imagine how a mother at the age of 42, with two kids still in grade school – and who hadn't taken care of the family finances or worked for pay in 16 years – had to retrofit her life to accommodate the changes from the death of her husband?

And that's no isolated case. Many people I counsel have one spouse or the other who is the more financially oriented. And it isn't gender-specific anymore. There are many husbands who defer to their wives because the latter are more adept at handling the family budget and often the investments that bolster that budget.

Times are different now and most couples have the wherewithal to handle the changes wrought by a death in the family. But they are not prepared generally to deal with the emotional issues that can cripple them while tending to these difficult tasks. My resolve was to create a process that can help individuals, families and businesses get through such transitional periods so that those who remain can live vital and productive lives.

Our process is meant to see clients during their lifetimes and make it easier, and ultimately less expensive, at settlement by establishing reasonable fees in advance so they know what to expect. Most clients don't realize they will have to pay something to a lawyer when someone they love dies. They go into a lawyer's office after that death, they are emotionally distraught, and after the lawyer tells them what needs to be done, he quotes a fee for the work. Sometimes it's hourly but to me that is like an open-ended contract with the lawyer.

Basically, the lawyer is saying "I don't know how long this will take me, but whatever the bill is, we expect you will pay it." What is the client to say at that point? "No"? I'm afraid I have to endorse the popular skepticism: Hourly fees reward the lawyer for taking more time – the more time the lawyer takes, the more they get paid.

It's much better if the client knows up front when times are calm what the fee structure is and then can decide – at the time of the settlement – whether they want to hire you or not. And we set up our system to know the current status of the assets, so usually it takes us less time to settle an estate than if we had not seen the client for 25 years.

Basically, at the end, it's a treasure hunt. The lawyer doesn't know how the assets are titled and relies on the client for that information. The lawyer needs to find the assets, figure out where they are to go and how to get them there. That takes time, and on an hourly basis, it can be financially devastating to clients.

Our process works well and clients are usually pleased with the outcome and the assistance they receive at this crucial point in their lives. So, by establishing a process that actually helps clients during their lifetimes, you set the stage for them to be taken care of after you are no longer running the firm – and essentially provide the funding to pay for your transition out!

If the annual revenue stream is coming in, and you have structured the transition carefully so that clients are pretty much guaranteed to stay with the firm – in part because you interact with them every year – this provides the revenue stream so that your interest in the business can be purchased.

CHAPTER 16
PLANNING YOUR OWN EXIT

As I get older, there are many younger clients I personally won't be able to help. Choosing a competent younger colleague to take over the practice is in line with promises made to clients, ensuring we can take care of their families when the need arises. So, in our practice, I have chosen a colleague who will work with me to make that transition happen.

My transition plan dictates that whoever takes over the practice will honor any existing contracts in a way that guarantees those families don't lose the benefit of the contract. Clients pay an annual fee to keep their plans maintained and update their planning as needs or the law change. That annual fee generates a certain portion of the annual revenues of the firm, and can also serve as the basis for the senior lawyer's exit strategy.

Essentially, by combining the revenues or two or more working lawyers, there are economies of scale so that the money coming in from the annual program exceeds what is necessary to run the firm and can actually serve as the buy-out for the senior lawyer without impacting the younger lawyer's revenue.

Most law firms, as the prior chapter noted, do not have a "going concern" value. When the senior lawyer dies, there is not much to sell. Revenues will stop or severely decline. In the alternative set forth here, the annual revenue creates a going-concern value and – depending on the number of people who are in the annual program – will create a value in excess of the annual revenues of the firm.

You can also consider buying a practice from an older lawyer and transitioning the existing client base from a transactional relationship to a maintenance-focused program. This may be more difficult for practices that are more transactional, like litigation, but if you can create a program that incorporates client relationship, and has a long-term element to it, you can make this work. In order to do that, you need to outline what services or benefits you will offer the clients and the fees you charge. It needs to be reasonable for the work to be done and within what the clients will be willing to pay.

I would recommend having someone in your office help you with the work related to the annual service program, but stay on top of what is being done so you preserve the client relationship until you are ready to make the transition. Be on the lookout for younger lawyers who have a similar philosophy to yours who would be interested in working together down the road as a transition strategy.

Certainly for new clients the new process will become part of your main offering. If you develop the strategy correctly, and you believe sincerely that the service you are offering will benefit the client, most of the new clients you meet will jump on board.

For existing clients, you can offer them a discount as "charter members" to get a core group into the program at the start. When it comes to the best way to inform existing clients of this new benefit, it will take some preparation and must be planned out. Perhaps you offer a meeting with the existing client base to roll out the program. Or you might try offering it to small groups in a more intimate setting. How well this works depends on the structure and demographic of your client base and the relationships you have been able to establish thus far.

If you buy out another lawyer's practice, you might be able to position it as a way for the older lawyer to gracefully exit the business in style, without being too much of a drain on your revenues. Each practice will be different and the appropriate methods and language may also depend on the area of the country you live in.

Still – with an exit plan properly thought-out and structured – you can assure significant enhancements for your client families and enterprises, make their lives better, and retire with the peace of mind that you have met the obligations your firm has stood by for years – and in some cases decades.

CHAPTER 17
WHAT'S NEXT?

Have you thought about what life would look like were you to retire? Think about it. You won't sit in a rocking chair, or be able to play golf or travel every week. Most people don't think systematically about the next chapter in their lives. But you could very well spend 20, 30 or 40 years in retirement.

You are a vital and creative individual and those juices don't stop running because you quit going to an office every day and aren't responsible for keeping a staff employed. What are your passions in life?

I have a good friend who is a busy executive for a major financial company. She works hard every day helping her team be the best and give the best to the stakeholders of her firm. But on the side, she helps the wounded coming home from Afghanistan and Iraq – men and women in our armed forces who have lost limbs and worse protecting our freedom. With others who work with her towards this lofty goal, she has helped raise millions of dollars to benefit those in the military. When you talk with her, her eyes light up when she speaks about her passion. Yes, she has a day job, but her passion lies with helping people in this distinctive way.

My friend is truly a unique individual, but your skills and aspirations are unique too. Think about what drives you passionately and makes you want to get up in the morning jazzed and effervescent. Maybe its community service, or helping children, or facilitating the physically challenged. Maybe it's sitting on the porch with your fishing pole teaching others to fly-fish.

Is there something that drives and excites you? If you find it, plan now for how you can attain that goal. Take courses that will help you achieve it. Perhaps it's consulting part-time in the field you specialized in while building the practice.

I have a friend that worked as a labor lawyer for a large Chicago firm for many years. He decided to retire at 60, then went to school for a degree in psychology. He then got his certification as a counselor to help lawyers and other professionals deal with the stresses of a practice and learn how to make their practices better. And he is more fulfilled than he has ever been. Working hard? You bet – but also loving every minute of it.

You can attain clarity on what compels you along with, in this emerging stage of your life, what will allow you to advance it in ways that are both productive and meaningful – and do that in a manner not unlike the spirit you showed when you launched your own practice.

Best of luck to you and yours, my friend. I appreciate your going along on the journey of this book; and I also hope the book sheds creative light on how much responsibility and opportunity awaits you, whether you are 28, 43, 58, or – well, pick just about any number.

APPENDIX
SYSTEMS, RULES AND HABITS:
THE FINER POINTS

I.   SETTING UP SYSTEMS

I found that having systems for just about every-thing is the most effective way to make governance easier. Not every practice can systematize processes, but here are the most productive among the systems we put in place...

a) A Client Management System

b) Client information

c) What additional information you will want to keep about your clients and the cases you are working on

d) A way to keep track of the marketing and networking you are doing so you can follow up

e) We have a system to get the physical production of cases we are working on completed in a timely fashion

    i) Gathering and securing confidential

information with clients

ii) Securing the computer systems in the office to avoid hacking and security breaches

iii)Conflicts resolution to keep within ethical standards

iv) Type of computer systems you want in the office

- One stand-alone computer

- Apple or PC

- An integrated computer system with routers and a network so that anyone on your team can access all the systems and any of the paperwork for any client

v) Organization of data

- Client correspondence

- Separate files for each case vs. one file

- A client or file numbering system

    1. This is critical. At first you will be happy for any file in the office. After a few years, the paper will

weigh you down and be impossible to keep up with. Establish an organization system that you can keep up with and use it religiously.

2. Train your staff on how to use it and make sure all of you are consistent. If your assistant files everything by first name, and you file by last name, it will be impossible to find the information you need easily.

3. Using a numbering system will help in two ways – first, it organizes things; second, it allows for expansion more easily as you get more files than finding things alphabetically. While filing alphabetically may be easier to find, as you grow you may wind up reorganizing the files for all the families with the last name starting in "S". Recognize that keeping paper copies will create a space problem.

4. Storage of data. With technology today, there is no lack of ways to store data, and it doesn't have to be

in hard paper files. Just make sure it is organized in a consistent way so you can retrieve the information you need in a timely way.

5. Have a check-out system for files by who has the file, whether it's in the office or in storage and whether it has been scanned.

I would keep track of the following, using any process you have that works:

II.   OPENING THE MAIL

III. CREATING LEGAL DOCUMENTS

a) Pleadings

b) Wills

c) Trusts

d) Ancillary Documents

e) Corporate and LLC documents

f) Correspondence

And the list goes on and on. The procedure should incorporate from start to finish how things are handled.

IV. AFTER MEETING AND RETAINING A CLIENT

a) Dictate a memo to the file outlining the major points of the conversation and what needs to be done next, by whom and when

b) Distribute the memo to the staff

c) Send out the engagement letter to the client (or better yet, have the client sign the engagement letter when they are in the office giving you a check for the retainer)

V.   SETTING UP THE FILE

a) Assign the file a client file number

b) Prepare the file label

c) Prepare the subfiles in the main client file

VI. CREATE A COMPUTER FILE FOR THE CLIENT ON THE SERVER

a) Scan in important papers to the clients' file

b) Organize the computer files consistently across the firm for each file opened

VII. FILE CREATION

In our office, we have written procedures for each type of file we create so that the staff and I know exactly how each file is to be created, the steps to be followed each time and the naming conventions to be used for each type of document created. This creates consistency among all the team in the office and will avoid costly wastes of time when looking for documents. For example, in our office we have procedures for...

a) Estate-Planning and Funding

   i) Estate-Planning Checklist

   ii) Advanced Planning Checklist

   iii)ILIT Checklist

   iv) GDOT Checklist

d) No matter what type of file is created, have someone be responsible for keeping the file in order, especially if you are not that type of person

VIII. FAMILY MEETINGS

a) What will the presentation look like

b) Who will be invited to attend

c) Agenda for the meeting

d) What set up needs to be done beforehand

   i) Files necessary

   ii) PowerPoint presentation

   iii) Handouts

   iv) Room set up and refreshments

IX. FUNDING ASSISTANCE PROCESSES

If you decide to assist in the funding of the trusts, define what services you will provide and the process you will use.

X.   GENERAL OFFICE

   a) Office décor and image/branding

   b) Using the CRM

   c) Creating Mailing lists and labels

   d) Using Mail merge

   e) Using proprietary document
       creation software

   f) Using accounting and payroll software

   g) Reviewing Documents

   h) Employee Paid Time-Off policy

   i) Annual days firm is closed for
       Federal holidays

XI.   PROCEDURES FOR USING
      VARIOUS SOFTWARE

Securely document passwords and any unique-
nesses about the software you use and keep the
copies of the software if it's not downloaded
handy in case your system goes down or you get
new computers.

XII. SEMINAR AND WORKSHOP SET-UP NOTES

If you put on seminars, I would outline the procedures you use, including...

a) When to book the venue

b) How and when to send invitations

c) Will you provide refreshments or not

d) How the venue tables will be set up

e) Will you need a projector and screen, flip charts, etc.

f) Who will be responsible for handling the RSVPs

g) Who will prepare the PowerPoint presentation